MACMILLAN ACADEMIC SKILLS

Skillful
Listening&Speaking

Teacher's Book

Foundation

Author: Louis Rogers
Series Consultant: Dorothy E. Zemach

CW00661284

Macmillan Education
4 Crinan Street
London N1 9XW
A division of Macmillan Publishers Limited
Companies and representatives throughout the world

ISBN 978-0-230-44345-7

Text, design and illustration © Macmillan Publishers 2013
Written by Louis Rogers

The author has asserted her rights to be identified as the author of this
work in accordance with the Copyright, Designs and Patents Act 1988.

First published 2013

All rights reserved; no part of this publication may be reproduced,
stored in a retrieval system, transmitted in any form, or by any means,
electronic, mechanical, photocopying, recording, or otherwise, without
the prior written permission of the publishers.

Note to Teachers

Photocopies may be made, for classroom use, of pages 88-97 without
the prior written permission of Macmillan Publishers Limited.
However, please note that the copyright law, which does not normally
permit multiple copying of published material, applies to the rest of
this book.

Designed by emc design ltd

Cover design by emc design ltd

Page layout by MPS Limited

The Academic Keyword List (AKL) was designed by Magali Paquot
at the Centre for English Corpus Linguistics, Université catholique de
Louvain (Belgium) within the framework of a research project led by
Professor Sylviane Granger.

http://www.uclouvain.be/en-372126.html

Author's acknowledgements

I'd like to thank everyone involved in the project for making *Skillful*
such a great series.

Please see Student's Book imprint page for visual walkthrough photo
credits. All author photos were kindly supplied by the authors.

The author and publishers are grateful for permission to reprint the
following copyright material:

Material from *The Study Skills Handbook* by author Stella Cottrell,
copyright © Stella Cottrell 1999, 2003 & 2008, first published by
Palgrave Macmillan, reproduced with permission of the publisher.

These materials may contain links for third party websites. We have
no control over, and are not responsible for, the contents of such third
party websites. Please use care when accessing them.

Although we have tried to trace and contact copyright holders before
publication, in some cases this has not been possible. If contacted
we will be pleased to rectify any errors or omissions at the earliest
opportunity.

Printed and bound in Thailand

2017 2016 2015 2014
10 9 8 7 6 5 4 3 2

Contents

		Listening texts	Listening skill	Vocabulary skill	Grammar
UNIT 1	Self Page 7	1 Nice to meet you 2 Student of the month	**Global** Listening for the main idea	Forming plurals	The verb *be*
UNIT 2	Family Page 17	1 Tell me about your family 2 All in the family	**Close** Listening for details	Organizing words: diagrams	Possessive adjectives
UNIT 3	Stuff Page 27	1 Something special 2 Get organized	**Pre-listening** Activating prior knowledge	Identifying parts of speech in a dictionary	Possessive pronouns
UNIT 4	Money Page 37	1 Can I help you? 2 Weekend sales	**Close** Listening for numbers	Using synonyms	Demonstrative pronouns: *this, that, these, those*
UNIT 5	Taste Page 47	1 Mealtime habits 2 Street food	**Close** Listening for times	Changing nouns to adjectives by adding *-y*	Simple present tense
UNIT 6	Play Page 57	1 A typical day 2 What a hobby!	**Close** Making inferences	Collocating with *go, play,* and *do*	Prepositions of time: *in, at, on*
UNIT 7	Places Page 67	1 Is it far? 2 New to Australia	**Close** Listening for and following directions	Writing definitions	*Can*
UNIT 8	Fun Page 77	1 I miss that show! 2 The fun theory	**Close** Listening to confirm predictions	Recognizing homophones	*So* and *neither*
UNIT 9	Plans Page 87	1 My plans 2 Are you free?	**Close** Listening for reasons	Forming compound nouns	Verb + infinitive
UNIT 10	Celebration Page 97	1 Thanksgiving 2 Songkran	**Close** Taking notes while listening	Identifying word families	Quantifiers

Speaking skill	Pronunciation skill	Speaking task	Digibook video activity	Study skills
Asking for repetition	Plural endings	Interviewing a classmate	Campus life	Understanding classroom language
Asking follow-up questions	Syllables	Presenting your family tree	Around the dinner table	Working with others
Asking what something is called	Word stress	Talking about everyday items	Messy desk, messy mind	Creating a vocabulary notebook
Talking about prices	Intonation in questions	Role-playing a shopping situation	At the shops	What are my personal resources?
Asking for clarification	Sentence stress	Describing a favorite meal or snack	Eat out or eat in?	Using a learner's dictionary
Reacting appropriately	Intonation patterns in reactions	Interviewing a classmate about free time	Taking hobbies to the extreme	Doing a web search
Using signal words to order information	Linking sounds	Describing and giving directions to a place	In the city	Current skills and qualities
Expressing likes and dislikes	Stress in responses	Discussing likes and dislikes	Time for vacation!	Prioritizing tasks
Making, accepting, and declining invitations	Reduction of *have to*	Inviting people to do things with you	Career choices	Emphasis on action!
Summarizing information	Reduction of *of* after quantifiers	Presenting about a special day	In celebration of food	Dealing with exam stress

Visual walkthrough

VOCABULARY PREVIEW Pre-teaching essential vocabulary which appears in both texts within the unit.

BEFORE YOU LISTEN These introductions to the listening topics prepare students for the upcoming subject matter.

GLOBAL LISTENING
Global listening is the first time the students hear the text; encouraging them to engage with the big issues and the overall picture before moving on to a more detailed analysis.

SKILLS BOXES These focus on new skills, giving information on why they are important and how to do them. They also highlight the linguistic features to look out for.

SENTENCE FRAMES Add support and help for students who lack confidence with their speaking skills.

LISTENING TASKS Providing the opportunity to put a new skill into practice.

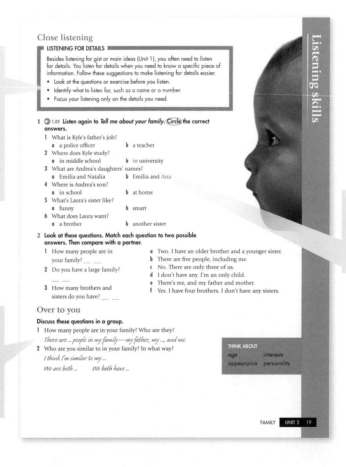

Listening skills

Vocabulary preview 1

1 Look at the picture of the Nomura family. Complete the sentences with the words from the box. Then compare with a partner.

| brother | daughter | father | husband |
| mother | sister | son | wife |

1 Yoshi is Fumi's _____.
2 Haru is Junko's _____.
3 Junko is Yoshi's _____.
4 Junko is Haru's _____.
5 Fumi is Haru's _____.
6 Fumi is Yoshi's _____.
7 Haru is Fumi's _____.
8 Yoshi is Junko's _____.

I think the answer to number 1 is ...   What do you think?

2 Work with a new partner. Make true or false sentences about the Nomura family. Your partner says *That's true* or *That's false*.

A: Yoshi is Junko's brother.
B: That's false. Yoshi is Junko's husband.

LISTENING 1 Tell me about your family

Before you listen
Look at the three pictures below. Describe each one. Use the words in the *Vocabulary preview*.
In this picture, there are two parents and ...
In this picture, there is one ...

Global listening

1.09 Listen to three people talking about their families. Number the pictures from 1 to 3.

Close listening

LISTENING FOR DETAILS

Besides listening for gist or main ideas (Unit 1), you often need to listen for details. You listen for details when you need to know a specific piece of information. Follow these suggestions to make listening for details easier.
• Look at the questions or exercise before you listen.
• Identify what to listen for, such as a name or a number.
• Focus your listening only on the details you need.

1 1.09 Listen again to *Tell me about your family.* Circle the correct answers.
1 What is Kyle's father's job?
  a a police officer   b a teacher
2 Where does Kyle study?
  a in middle school   b in university
3 What are Andrea's daughters' names?
  a Emilia and Natalia   b Emilia and Ana
4 Where is Andrea's son?
  a in school   b at home
5 What's Laura's sister like?
  a funny   b smart
6 What does Laura want?
  a a brother   b another sister

2 Look at these questions. Match each question to two possible answers. Then compare with a partner.
1 How many people are in your family? ___ ___
2 Do you have a large family? ___ ___
3 How many brothers and sisters do you have? ___ ___

  a Two. I have an older brother and a younger sister.
  b There are five people, including me.
  c No. There are only three of us.
  d I don't have any. I'm an only child.
  e There's me, and my father and mother.
  f Yes. I have four brothers. I don't have any sisters.

Over to you

Discuss these questions in a group.
1 How many people are in your family? Who are they?
  There are ... people in my family—my father, my ..., and me.
2 Who are you similar to in your family? In what way?
  I think I'm similar to my ...
  We are both ...   We both have ...

THINK ABOUT
age   interests
appearance   personality

Listening skills

SPEAKING Presenting your family tree

You are going to learn about possessive adjectives and syllables in words. You are then going to use these skills to present your family tree.

Grammar

POSSESSIVE ADJECTIVES

We use the possessive adjectives *my, your, his, her, its, our,* and *their* to show who owns ("possesses") something. Possessive adjectives are followed by a noun.
Yoshi's wife is Junko.   *His* wife is Junko.
The parents' children are Haru and Fumi.   *Their* children are Haru and Fumi.
Don't confuse possessive adjectives with other structures.

Possessive adjectives	Subject pronoun + be	
your	you're (= you are)	You're name is Billy. ✗
his	he's (= he is)	
its	it's (= it is)	
their	they're (= they are)	

1 Circle the correct possessive adjective.
1 Here's a picture of my niece. **Her / His** name is Aicha.
2 Nora and Cal are married. **Her / Their** daughter is one year old.
3 I love to watch TV. **My / Its** favorite show is *Family X*.
4 We go to Jefferson College. **My / Our** school is fantastic.
5 **Our / Your** parents are so nice. Do you live with them?
6 I have a new car. **My / Its** color is dark blue.
7 Jason loves **his / her** grandmother. He often visits her.

2 Complete the conversation with the correct possessive adjectives. Then compare and practice with a partner.
A: Is that a new phone?
B: Yeah. (1) _____ camera is really nice. Here, look at (2) _____ family pictures. Here's (3) _____ brother, Rob. We're in front of (4) _____ house. We share a room.
A: Nice. And who's that? Is that (5) _____ sister?
B: No, that's (6) _____ niece. And that's (7) _____ brother—so, of course, he's (8) _____ nephew.
A: What are (9) _____ names?
B: Amy and Patrick. Look! Here's one of me and (10) _____ parents.
A: What's (11) _____ father's name?
B: Ken. And (12) _____ mother's name is Kathleen.

3 Work in a group. Do you have any pictures of family or friends on your cell phone? Tell your classmates about them.

FAMILY UNIT 2 23

SECTION OVERVIEW Giving students the context within which they are going to study the productive skills.

GRAMMAR BOX Providing notes on form and function. The text assumes prior exposure to the language.

REAL-WORLD FOCUS The focus on real-world situations allows students to use these skills in discussion groups and seminars.

AUDIO MATERIALS Providing guided practice.

Speaking skill

EXPRESSING LIKES AND DISLIKES

Look at these different ways we can express likes and dislikes.

Likes	Dislikes
I like ...	I don't like ...
I like ... very much / a lot.	I don't like ... very much / at all.
I love ...	I hate ...

A noun, infinitive, or gerund can follow the verbs *like, love,* and *hate.*
I like **TV**. (noun)   I love **to watch TV**. (infinitive)   I hate **watching TV**. (gerund)

1 Put the words in order to make sentences.
1 a lot / likes / Luke / reality shows / .
2 like / I / sitcoms / don't / at all / .
3 hate / game shows / I / watching / .
4 very much / doesn't / watching / Rex / like / TV / .
5 loves / TV shows / to / Shannon / download / .
6 like / novels / I / reading / very much / .

2 How do you feel about these things? Write true sentences using *love, like, don't like,* or *hate.*
1 to watch sports shows _____
2 documentaries _____
3 listening to the radio _____
4 talk shows _____
5 reading magazines _____
6 speaking English _____

Pronunciation skill

STRESS IN RESPONSES

Notice which words are stressed in these responses.

	Feel same way	Feel different way
I love talk shows.	**So** do I.	Oh? **I** don't.
I don't like sitcoms.	**Neither** do I.	Really? **I** do.

1 🔊 2.22 Underline the stressed words in the responses. Then listen and check your answers.
1 I don't like dramas at all.   Really? I do.
2 I love to read short stories.   So do I.
3 I don't like to stay out late.   Neither do I.
4 I like to play chess.   Oh? I don't.

2 Work with a partner. Take turns reading your sentences from *Speaking skill* exercise 2, and responding.
A: *I don't like to watch sports shows.*   B: *Neither do I.*

84 UNIT 8 FUN

SPEAKING TASK

Read this discussion. Circle the things the speakers say they like or don't like. Underline responses where someone feels the same way. Double underline the responses where someone feels a different way.
A: Let's watch TV. Sound good?
B: Sure. What do you want to watch?
A: How about *Sunday Nights Sports*? I love that show.
B: Really? I don't. I find it boring. But I love to watch soccer.
A: So do I. But there's no soccer on—just baseball.
C: *Life with Mickey* is on. I like that show.
A: Oh? I don't. I don't find it funny at all. But I like that reality show *Super Student.*
C: So do I.
B: Can we watch a documentary? I see that *Extreme Journeys* is on. I love that show.
C: I don't like it at all. Sorry.
A: Neither do I.
B: It's not easy to agree on anything.
C: Why don't we go outside and do something? We can go to the park.

BRAINSTORM
List one thing you like and don't like in each category.

	Like	Don't like
Sport or game		
TV show or movie		
Book or magazine		
Actor or musician		
Food or drink		
School subject or class		
Other:		

PLAN
Look at your brainstorm and decide how much you like or don't like each thing. Plan to discuss each one.

SPEAK
Work in a group. Take turns discussing your likes and dislikes. Pay attention to the word stress in your responses.

SHARE
Work with a different partner. Tell your partner five things you remember from your group discussion. Your partner responds.

FUN UNIT 8 85

SKILLS BOXES Highlighting pronunciation advice.

GUIDED PRACTICE Guides students through the stages of a speaking task.

VISUAL WALKTHROUGH 7

STUDY SKILLS WITH STELLA COTTRELL

Information on study skills features at the end of every unit. Some of these pages showcase a task from Stella Cottrell's bestselling title *The Study Skills Handbook*.

STUDY TIPS
Stella offers students useful and memorable tips to improve their studying methods through self-reflection and critiquing.

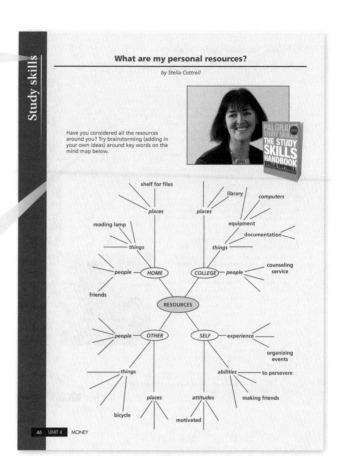

STUDY SKILLS SCENARIOS
Using original material, the other end-of-unit study skills task gives students a scenario to work through. This provides them with the opportunity for personal performance reflection.

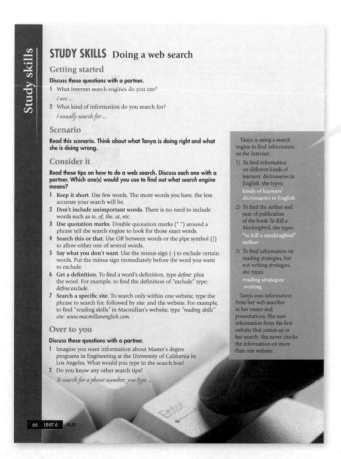

SKILLFUL VERSATILITY Both student and teacher facing, the *Skillful* Digibook can be used for group activities in the classroom, on an interactive whiteboard, or by the student alone for homework and extra practice.

DIGIBOOK TOOLBAR The toolbar that appears on each page allows for easy manipulation of the text. Features such as highlighting and a text tool for commenting allow the teacher to add points as the class goes along, and functions like the zoom and grab tool mean the teacher can focus students' attention on the appropriate sections.

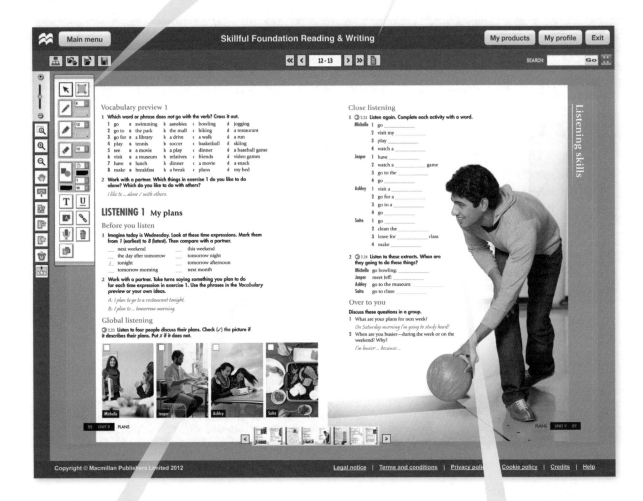

EMBEDDED AUDIO For instant access to the audio for unit exercises, the Digibook has embedded files that you can reach in one click.

PAGE-FAITHFUL Provides a digital replica of the *Skillful* Student's Books while hosting additional, interactive features.

WHAT IS *SKILLFUL* PRACTICE? The *Skillful* practice area is a student-facing environment designed to encourage extra preparation, and provides additional activities for listening, vocabulary, grammar, speaking, and pronunciation as well as support videos for listening and alternative unit assignments.

UNIT AND TASK SELECTION
Handy drop-down menus allow students to jump straight to their practice unit and the exercise they want to concentrate on.

TEACHER RESOURCES The *Skillful* teachers have many more resources at their fingertips.

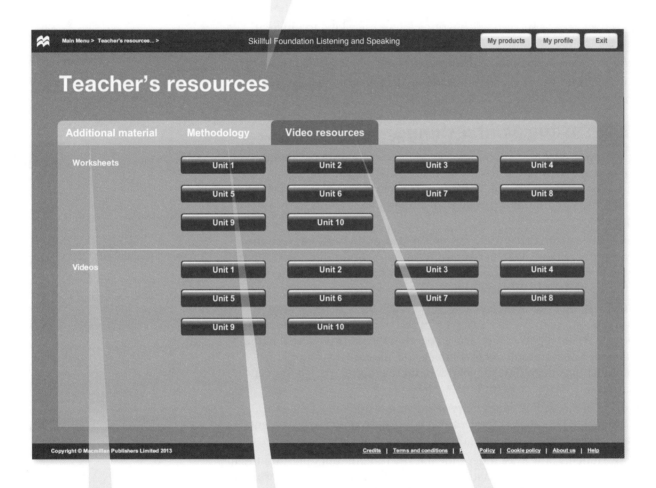

ADDITIONAL MATERIAL Along with the student add-ons there are printable worksheets, test materials, and a markbook component to grade and monitor student progress.

METHODOLOGY For teachers who may need a little extra help to effectively utilize all of the resources *Skillful* has to offer, there are course methodology notes.

VIDEO RESOURCES Teachers have access to the same videos as the students, and to complement these there are printable video worksheets to aid lesson planning.

To the teacher

Academic success requires so much more than memorizing facts. It takes skills. This means that a successful student can both learn and think critically. *Skillful* helps teachers prepare their students for academic work in English by teaching not only language—vocabulary and grammar—but the necessary skills to engage with topics, texts, and discourse with classmates.

Skillful gives students:

- engaging texts on a wide variety of topics, each examined from two different academic disciplines
- skills for learning about a wide variety of topics from different angles and from different academic areas
- skills they need to succeed when reading and listening to these texts
- skills they need to succeed when writing for and speaking to different audiences
- skills for critically examining the issues presented by a speaker or a writer
- study skills for learning and remembering the English language and important information.

Teachers using *Skillful* should:

- Encourage students to ask questions and interact. Learning a language is not passive. Many of the tasks and exercises involve pairwork, groupwork, and whole-class discussion. Working with others helps students solidify their understanding, and challenge and expand their ability to think critically.
- Personalize the material. Help students make connections between the texts in their book and their own world—home, community, and country. Bring in outside material from local sources when it's relevant, making sure it fits the unit topics and language.
- Provide a lot of practice. Have students do each exercise several times, with different partners. Review exercises and material from previous units. Use the *Skillful* digital component to develop the skills presented in the Student's Book. Have students complete the additional activities on a computer outside of class to make even more progress. Assign frequent manageable review tasks for homework.
- Provide many opportunities for review. Remind students of the skills, grammar, and vocabulary they learned in previous units. Have students study a little bit each day, not just before tests.
- Show students how to be independent learners. Point out opportunities to study and practice English outside of class, such as reading for pleasure and using the Internet in English. Have them find and share information about the different unit topics with the class. The *Study skills* section in every unit gives students valuable tips for successfully managing their own learning.

Learning skills, like learning a language, takes time and practice. Students must be patient with themselves as they put in the necessary time and effort. They should set and check goals. Periodic assessments the teacher can print, such as the unit tests, progress tests, and end test on the digital component let students see their own progress and measure how much they've learned, so they can feel proud of their academic and linguistic development.

The *Skillful* blend by Dorothy E. Zemach

In some academic disciplines, students can begin by acquiring a lot of facts and general knowledge. In a language, however, students need far more than information—they need skills. They need to know how to do things: how to explain, persuade, ask for help, extend an invitation, outline and argue a thesis, distinguish between important and unimportant information, follow digressions, understand implied information, and more.

Skillful recognizes that skills such as these can't be learned by memorizing facts. To acquire these skills, students must notice them as they read or listen; break them down and understand them through clear explanations; and then rehearse and apply those skills in carefully scaffolded activities that lead to freer practice.

The listening and reading texts in each unit introduce students to one subject area explored through two different academic disciplines and two distinct genres. Students learn and practice both global skills, such as recognizing tone and identifying the main idea, and close skills, such as understanding pronoun references and figuring out vocabulary from context, to understand the texts on several levels.

These days, students must interact with both digital and printed text, online and offline, in the classroom and in the workplace. The *Skillful* textbooks are therefore supplemented with the *Skillful* digital components. These further develop, explain, and extend the skills work found in the printed textbooks. They provide additional exercises related to the skills, the grammar points, and the vocabulary areas. They can be accessed either via the Digibook or through the *Skillful* practice area. Scores are tracked and recorded, and if students work offline, their markbook will be updated the next time they connect to the Internet.

Videos for each unit provide additional subject area content that review the skills and language taught in the unit. The videos can be shown in class to feed in additional content, and the accompanying worksheets can be used to structure the lesson.

Unit checklists help students keep track of language in the unit and review for tests.

The digital components also help teachers with classroom organization and management by assigning and tracking homework, and monitoring student progress using the markbook. A full suite of test materials can be used for placement into the appropriate level, and then provide end-of-unit tests and end-of-course tests that can be used as both formative assessments (to evaluate progress) and summative assessments (to mark achievements and assign grades). Tests are provided in both editable and non-editable formats enabling teachers to manipulate the content, as desired. The format of these tests is similar to internationally recognized standardized tests.

Dorothy E. Zemach taught ESL for over 18 years, in Asia, Africa, and the U.S. She holds an MA in TESL, and now concentrates on writing and editing ELT materials and conducting teacher training workshops. Her areas of specialty and interest are teaching writing, teaching reading, business English, academic English, and testing.

Teaching study skills by Stella Cottrell

There is a growing awareness that students' performance, even in higher education, can be improved through training in relevant academic skills. Hurley (1994) described study skills as "key skills for all areas of education, including advanced study" and argued that students benefit when these skills are taught explicitly. In other words, it should not be assumed that the skills a student brings from school, or even from the first year of university, are sufficient to carry them through their degree. Skills such as task management, working with others, and critical thinking need to be fine-tuned and extended as students move from one level to another.

Globally, universities and colleges are giving far more attention to preparatory support for prospective students and to developing study skills once a student is on a programme. In some countries, there is a growing emphasis, too, on "employability skills," from soft skills such as communication, creativity, and working collaboratively to new attributes sought by employers, including business acumen, cross-cultural sensitivity, and enterprise. In addition, each institution tends to identify a range of skills and qualities that it wants to see embodied by its graduates.

One of the challenges is articulating what is meant by study skills in this changing environment. This has significance for students when trying to make sense of long lists of skills that they are expected to accumulate during their time in higher education. It also has a bearing on who teaches and supports study skills. In some colleges and universities, this falls to study skills specialists; in others, it may be allocated to teaching staff. In each case, different approaches are used to make sense of the learning experience.

From the students' perspective, it helps to organize study skills into a few, relatively easy-to-remember categories. In the latest version of *The Study Skills Handbook*, I suggest using four basic categories:

1 Self   2 Academic   3 People   4 Task

The starting place for students is being able to manage themselves within a new learning environment with confidence and resilience. They need to understand the rationale for, and benefits of, independent study and the kinds of challenges that they will be set. This involves organizing their time, coping with deadlines, and recognizing what it means to take charge of their own learning. It also includes metacognitive skills in reflecting on how they think, learn, and manage themselves for study.

Academic skills consist of such skills as the core research skills (finding, recording, and using information); thinking skills (critical thinking skills, creative problem-solving, and synthesis); understanding academic conventions (the nature and integrity of academic study); and writing skills.

People skills are increasingly important as collaborative study becomes a feature of higher education. These include such skills as giving and receiving criticism, supporting others without cheating, group project work, and playing an active role in group sessions. These can be an especial challenge for international students who may be used to different kinds of learning interactions.

Task management skills within this learning context include such skills as meeting given requirements, and using appropriate protocols and project management in order to achieve a given academic task such as writing an essay or report, undertaking research, conducting an experiment, or solving a problem.

An additional value of this framework is that the basic shell can be easily adapted to other contexts, such as employability. The "Self / People / Tasks" model is one that I used, for example, within *Skills for Success: Personal Development and Employability* (2010).

Stella Cottrell is Director for Lifelong Learning at the University of Leeds, U.K. She is author of the bestselling *The Study Skills Handbook, The Palgrave Student Planner, The Exam Skills Handbook, Critical Thinking Skills, Study Skills Connected*, and *Skills for Success*, all published by Palgrave Macmillan.

Reference
Hurley, J. (1994), *Supporting Learning* (Bristol: The Staff College and Learning Partners).

Teaching academic vocabulary by Pete Sharma

It has been estimated that in an academic text, a quarter of the words are either "academic vocabulary" or "technical vocabulary." What is "academic vocabulary"? The term includes:

- concepts, such as *research*
- actions, such as *classifying* and *defining*
- nouns, such as *sources* and *references*
- collocations, such as *reading list*, and
- reporting language, such as *argue*.

Academic vocabulary is used across all disciplines. This essay will describe a range of activities for teaching academic vocabulary.

Students meet and practice new vocabulary in every kind of lesson, and especially in reading and listening lessons. In a listening lesson, you may pre-teach key vocabulary before students do the listening task. Similarly, in a reading lesson, you can pre-teach specific words to make the text easier to read. Throughout the *Skillful* Student's Book, there are "Vocabulary skill" boxes. Giving presentations provides opportunities for students to use and practice new vocabulary, and for you to provide feedback on their pronunciation. Similarly, writing essays allows learners to produce the new words they have learned in context.

During the course, you will not only present and practice vocabulary, but also give advice on effective learning strategies. Explore the different ways students can record the new vocabulary they meet on the course. Many students merely jot down a word and write a translation next to it, so it is helpful to present alternatives, such as creating "word trees." Have students work together to create mind-maps on relevant topics, as we remember words when we meet them in concept groups. The *Skillful* Teacher's Book includes several ideas for using a vocabulary notebook. Point out that many words have a standard meaning and an academic meaning. Give examples: references; argument. Students frequently start their academic course over-using their bilingual dictionary. They benefit from a lesson or lessons exploring the pros and cons of using a monolingual, English–English dictionary. A good way to start a dictionary lesson is to do a quiz to show some useful dictionary features in the dictionary. Part of a lesson can be spent introducing learners to electronic dictionaries, which allow students to listen to new words. You can demonstrate a CD-ROM and web-based dictionary using a data projector. There are several important features of academic vocabulary that you will wish to focus on during the course. It is useful to provide practice on prefixes and suffixes, since noticing patterns in the language can help learners work out the meaning of new words. Also, focus on "collocation" or "word partnerships." Before students read a text, you can select some key collocations, write them on cards, and get students to match them. Students can then scan the text and highlight these collocations before moving to more intensive reading practice. There are several language exercises on prefixes, suffixes, and collocations in *Skillful,* and the Teacher's Book also contains sets of photocopiable cards which can be used in many ways, as warmers, for example, or for reviewing lexis. There is no need to develop a new methodology for teaching academic vocabulary. Good practice involves students meeting new words in context, practicing them in speaking and writing, and recycling them in a variety of ways. Working through the units and different levels of *Skillful* will enable students to practice and review academic vocabulary systematically.

Pete Sharma is an associate Lecturer at Oxford Brookes University, U.K. He has written books on technology in language teaching, and is co-author of *Blended Learning* (Macmillan: 2007) and *400 Ideas for Interactive Whiteboards* (Macmillan: 2010).

English for Academic Purposes (EAP) in the twenty-first century by Gary Pathare

Gone are the days when learning English was an optional leisure pursuit, consisting of unhurried progression through the levels from beginner to advanced. Competence was generally tested through informal tests or by external general English exams. In the new paradigm, however, learning English is not recreation. It has become a serious business which may significantly affect learners' lives through improved career or educational prospects. An EAP course needs to take this fully into account.

The recent major changes can be traced to three main factors; the examination process, the advent of the digital age, and changes in the cultural role of English.

EAP exams

The success of exams like the Academic version of the IELTS is testament to the fact that EAP is a major growth area. The current popularity of these exams is largely due to the fact that they are used as gatekeepers to higher education conducted in English. To be effective, these exams have to be rigorous and fair. Any EAP course nowadays has to take into account the likelihood that the learners will have to prove themselves in this arena, and must fully address the skill and strategy requirements of the exam to be taken.

Technology

The next great change relates to technology. The twenty-first century is the digital age. Multi-media devices have become commonplace, and in some contexts the pen is being superseded by the computer. This has obviously impacted EAP, especially in the developed world. In many settings, a blended learning approach is taken, in which a combination of online and book-based learning is used. Some language-learning tasks are performed on a computer, and "instant" research is possible, an obvious benefit in an academic environment. Another critical change resulting from the digital revolution has been the development of corpus linguistics, derived from information collected in computer databases. Researchers and coursebook writers now have easy access to accurate data about how academic English is actually used. This particularly affects vocabulary learning, where academic words have been identified, as well as other areas such as functional language.

Global English

Another significant change is the recognition that English in the twenty-first century is a global phenomenon. EAP course materials have to be appropriate to markets as culturally diverse as China and Saudi Arabia. This daunting task is achieved in courses like *Skillful* by drawing on research into the common core of academic English skills and language, putting it into contexts that are multi-cultural and balanced, rather than Anglo-centric. The resulting classroom is a more interesting one, in which there is room for exploration of cultural diversity, especially when coupled with the opportunities for global research afforded by the digital revolution.

Implications for teachers

What is the teacher to make of this? An awareness of the language and skills required for the academic exams is vital, and these must be introduced, recycled, and structured effectively. It certainly helps to use a coursebook such as *Skillful* which has been developed with a deep understanding of the requirements of the academic context, which may be used as an entire course or as a core to be supplemented. The main challenge for the twenty-first century EAP teacher, however, is to make sure that the English classroom remains a place in which language development is not supplanted by exam strategy work, and where language learning remains enjoyable even when the stakes are high.

Gary Pathare (M.Ed. TESOL, University of Newcastle) has taught English for over 20 years, and, since 2001, has taught EAP to students in the United Arab Emirates. He is a teacher trainer, a senior writer for the UAE university entrance exam, and a winner of the UAE IT Challenge. Gary also writes ESL books and materials for international publishers, as well as for his own teaching context. He regularly presents at international conferences, and publishes articles on topics including teaching spelling, reading and vocabulary, innovative uses of technology, teacher training, and independent learning.

Developing listening skills by Emma Pathare

Listening presents many challenges for second language learners and for their teachers, and it is often felt to be one of the most difficult of the four skills to deal with. Asking questions helps us to see the surrounding issues, and these questions can guide us in further research of the subject. Here are six questions to get you started.

What do your students need to listen to in their academic life?

Students have to deal with both face-to-face (e.g., tutor groups) and remote situations (e.g., listening to podcasts) in their academic lives. Each situation brings its own expectations: should students respond, participate, or only listen? Thinking about this will help you to select useful classroom listening materials.

Why do students need to listen?

They need to understand, of course. But what do they need to understand? The general gist, the main ideas, or two or three specific details? Do they need to correct or confirm information, or even decide whether the information is relevant in the first place? The answers to these questions will indicate the task types your students need as they listen. The issue of response is again key. Will students engage in discussion, ask questions, take notes, or summarize? The answers here will help to determine the type of tasks to set students.

What difficulties do students have with listening?

A major factor is the "real time" nature of listening. The speed and immediacy can put a lot of pressure on the listener. Spoken language is often unpredictable, and the grammar and vocabulary can diverge from the often more formal language of written texts. Redundant language is also common. Raising awareness of these issues can build students' confidence, and smaller tasks focusing on grammar and pronunciation will help to build students' skills.

What is the purpose of listening in the English classroom?

Listening can, of course, be used to develop listening skills, but also it can be used for language input, where the end goal is less about improving listening, and more about developing grammar or vocabulary knowledge, for example. Listening is also used for content input, that is, to learn information.

The click of the "start" button, in many classrooms, however, is sometimes less to do with the concept of development or input, and more about practice or testing. It is true, students need extensive practice in listening, and we are fortunate nowadays, with global media and the Internet, that there is almost unlimited authentic material available for students to engage with. Testing, too, is important, and, if it is required, there are many specifically written materials available for teachers and students to use. As teachers, however, we need to make sure that valuable class time is primarily focused on developing listening skills and providing valuable input.

How does a skills-based approach help students?

A skills-based approach recognizes that the listening process, as a whole, encompasses a number of sub-skills. As listeners in our first language, we rarely focus on the more micro or "Close" skills, and we rely on the more top-down or "Global" skills of using world knowledge and knowledge of discourse structure to make sense of what we are listening to. Lower-level language learners, however, need explicit work on both types of skill.

How can you continue your development as a listening teacher?

The simple and practical answer is to continue the discussion. Take these questions, add your own, and bring them into your staffroom. Have discussions with your colleagues. Talk to the students. What do they think? Read up on current research. Share your findings. Keep exploring and asking questions.

Emma Pathare has taught ESL for over 17 years in Europe and the Middle East. She was the winner of the 2008 British Council ELTons award with "The Vocabulary Course," which grew out of the dissertation for her M.Ed. in ELT and Educational Technology. She now concentrates on material writing, both for international publishers and also for specific contexts in the UAE, where she is based.

Listening	Listening for the main idea
Vocabulary	Forming plurals
Grammar	The verb *be*
Speaking	Asking for repetition
Pronunciation	Plural endings

As this might be the first class for everyone, start with an ice breaker so that students can get to know each other. Write the answers to some basic questions on the board. For example: *My name is Mohammed. I am from Dubai. I like watching soccer and playing computer games. I study Economics. I want to be a banker.*

Ask students what questions were asked to get these answers. Write their suggestions on the board. (Answers: *What's your (first) name? Where are you from? What do you like doing in your free time? / What are your hobbies? What do you study? What do you want to be? / What job do you want to have?*) Next, ask students to work with a partner to ask and answer these questions. Ask individual students to report back to the class. Don't forget to introduce yourself and discuss the course objectives and the goals for Unit 1 before delving into the first *Discussion point* section.

Remember that at any stage, either in- or out of class, the students can access the *Skillful* digital component through the access codes in their Student's Book. Teachers can also access extra items such as tests through the access codes in the Teacher's Book. In the digital component, both students and teachers can also find the Digibook. This is a page-faithful representation of the Student's Book. It could be projected onto a screen such as an interactive whiteboard.

Discussion point

Ask students to look at the picture on page 7. Tell them that the people on the left are all important people in the life of the person on the right. Write on the board: *People in my life* and draw lines coming from the phrase. Write some examples on a few of the lines, such as *teacher*, *mother*, and *cousin*. Ask students to think of other important people in the person's life. You will probably get words such as *father*, *grandfather*, *sister*, *friends*, *classmates*, etc.

Ask students to discuss the questions with a partner, using the sentence frames to help them get started. After they have discussed the questions, ask one or two students to share their answers with the class. Point to the *Top baby names in 2013* box and ask students if they can add any more. You may want to practice the pronunciation of some of the names in the box.

Vocabulary preview 1

1   Write a made-up name on the board to show examples of all of the words in the box. Ask the class to label the names using the words from the box.

Then ask the students to complete the introduction with the words in the box.

ANSWERS		
1 full		5 title
2 first		6 short for
3 middle		7 initials
4 family		8 nickname

2   Ask students to work with a partner to discuss the questions. To extend the activity, talk about the meaning and origin of some family names.

Cultural awareness

Many Anglo-Saxon family names were originally connected to the jobs people did, such as Baker, Butcher, and Smith (blacksmith, goldsmith, etc.). Other common family names are connected to geographical features or place names, such as Hill. Others originate from the family itself; for example, names such as Johnson would originally have meant "son of John," etc.

LISTENING 1   Nice to meet you

Before you listen

Highlight the *Possible information* box to students. Ask them to discuss which information they would or would not give when first meeting someone. Ask for suggestions about other things they might discuss with different people, for example, a business colleague of your father.

Global listening

Generate a discussion about what types of things students listen to in their own language and have listened to in English. Elicit what they find hard or easy about listening to English. Explain the difference between global and close listening, and emphasize that both skills are valuable. Ask a student to read the *Listening for the main idea* box aloud.

Ask why it is important to listen for the main idea and not to focus on every word. Then ask students to listen and circle the main idea.

ANSWERS			
1 c	2 b	3 a	4 c

AUDIO SCRIPT   1.02

Eve: Hello. My name is Eve Bridges. I'm a student here at Jefferson High School. I like school, but I have a lot of other interests, too. I'm very interested in technology. I like computers a lot. I have three: a desktop at home, a laptop for school, and a tablet just for fun. I like to create web pages for my friends. I have a blog, too. I write about my favorite movies, music, TV shows—things like that.

Richard: Hi everyone. My name is Richard Hudson. But please just call me Rich. I study engineering. I'm from Dallas, Texas. I have a large family. I have two brothers and three sisters. One brother lives in Houston, and the other lives in New York. All of my sisters still live in Texas. Two of them are married and starting their own families. A large family is a lot of fun. Oh, by the way, I'm single.

Min-ki: Hello. My name is Park Min-ki. I'm from South Korea. Park is my family name. Family names come first in Korea. My nickname is Kevin. My hometown is Daejeon. Daejeon is a city in the middle of Korea. It's a pretty big city. I like my hometown a lot. It has good food, nice parks, and friendly people. Come visit me sometime!

Maria: Hello. My name is María. Well, my full name is María Conchita Gracia López. María is my first name, Conchita is my middle name, and my last names, or family names, are Gracia López. That's Gracia from my dad and López from my mom. It's common to have three or four names in Mexico. My parents call me María Conchita, but please just call me María. It's nice to meet you.

Close listening

1   Ask students to discuss what they remember about the people on the audio. Then play the audio again and ask them to do the exercise.

ANSWERS

1 a   2 b   3 a   4 b   5 b   6 a   7 b   8 b

2   Ask students to listen and complete the excerpts. Then you could ask them to adapt one of the excerpts so that it's about them.

AUDIO SCRIPT   1.03

Eve: Hello. My name is Eve Bridges. I'm a student here at Jefferson High School. I like school, but I have a lot of other interests, too. I'm very interested in technology.

Richard: Hi everyone. My name is Richard Hudson. But please just call me Rich. I study engineering. I'm from Dallas, Texas. I have a large family.

Min-ki: Hello. My name is Park Min-ki. I'm from South Korea. Park is my family name. Family names come first in Korea. My nickname is Kevin.

Maria: Hello. My name is María. Well, my full name is María Conchita Gracia López. María is my first name, Conchita is my middle name, and my last names, or family names, are Gracia López.

ANSWERS

1 student	5 from
2 interests	6 first
3 call	7 full
4 study	8 last

If you have students going on to continue their studies in the U.K., Canada, or the U.S., you might want to make use of the information in the *Cultural awareness* box.

Cultural awareness

In the U.S., the word *college* can refer to any higher education institution. Typically, colleges are made up of different academic departments, and universities are made up of different colleges that are separate from each other. Both can offer degrees. In Canada and the U.K., colleges more typically offer vocational qualifications and cannot offer degrees. However, more traditional universities in the U.K., such as Oxford and Cambridge, follow a model similar to the U.S. model.

Over to you

This task could be a short discussion straight from the book or, with more confident classes, ask for more details. For example, if a student says their interest is reading, ask them to explain what they like about a book they are reading. Refer students to the *Common interests* box for ideas.

This is a good place to use the video resource *Campus life*. It is located in the Video resources section of the digital component. Alternatively, remind the students about the video so they can do this at home.

Vocabulary preview 2

1   Before having students complete this task, you could write your own favorite for each category in the box on the board and ask students to match the names/titles to the words from the box.

ANSWERS

1 app	5 book
2 TV show	6 author
3 color	7 comic book
4 actor	8 website

2   Ask students to discuss the questions with a partner. Refer students to the *Colors* box for help with question 1. With stronger groups, you might want to extend this task by getting students to say more about each category.

LISTENING 2 Student of the month

Before you listen

Refer students to the *Think about* box. Tell them about a website you like and explain what features in the box it has. Then ask students to work in groups to discuss the questions.

Global listening

Explain the idea of "student of the month." Elicit ideas about things that someone might have to do in order to win such an award and write any suggestions on the board. You may need to explain the word *major* to students. Then ask them to listen and number the topics in order.

AUDIO SCRIPT 1.04

Jeff: Hello. I'm a reporter for *Student Times*, our school newspaper. I'm interviewing some students for this month's "Student of the Month" column.

Matt: And you want to interview me?

Jeff: That's right. Are you free?

Matt: Yeah, I am.

Jeff: Great. What's your name?

Matt: My name's Matt.

Jeff: Is Matt short for Matthew?

Matt: Yes, it is. My friends call me Matt. My parents call me Matthew.

Jeff: What's your last name?

Matt: Searby.

Jeff: I'm sorry. Can you repeat that?

Matt: Searby. It's S-E-A-R-B-Y.

Jeff: What's your major?

Matt: Economics.

Jeff: What is your hometown? Where are you from?

Matt: I'm originally from Manchester. Manchester, England.

Jeff: Oh, you're British?

Matt: Yes, I am. And I'm a big fan of Manchester United. Soccer is my favorite sport.

Jeff: What are your other interests?

Matt: Other interests? Well, I love reading.

Jeff: What kinds of books do you like?

Matt: Let's see … I like short stories. And I love travel books. I don't really travel very much, but I like to *read* about travel.

Jeff: What about TV and movies?

Matt: I don't watch movies much, but I watch TV.

Jeff: Are you a fan of travel shows?

Matt: Oh, yes. And I watch the news, too. Um, listen, I need to get to class.

Jeff: OK. Thank you so much Matt for talking with me today.

ANSWERS

1 his name	4 sports
2 his major	5 books
3 his hometown	6 movies and TV shows

Close listening

1 Play the audio again and get students to write *T* or *F* next to each statement. Because this is the first listening task that focuses on spelling, you might want to dictate more names to the class to write down. If you are in a monolingual class, you could focus on commonly confused sounds, for example, *i* and *e* for Italian speakers, or *p* and *b* for Arabic speakers.

ANSWERS

1 F 2 T 3 F 4 T 5 T 6 F

---

2 To make this task more challenging, you could put all of the words onto cut-up pieces of paper or card. Give one set of words to each small group and ask them to use the words to create five questions that they heard in the interview.

ANSWERS

1 What's your major?
2 What is your hometown?
3 What are your other interests?
4 What kinds of books do you like?
5 Are you a fan of travel shows?

---

3 Play the audio for students to check their answers.

AUDIO SCRIPT 1.05

1 What's your major?
2 What is your hometown?
3 What are your other interests?
4 What kinds of books do you like?
5 Are you a fan of travel shows?

---

4 Ask students to ask and answer the questions in exercise 2 with a partner. Students could repeat this task with two or three partners before feeding back on the most interesting answers they heard. Alternatively, you could encourage students to practice manipulating the structures into a new set of questions, e.g., *What kinds of films do you like? Are you a fan of crime dramas?*

Over to you

Ask students to discuss the questions in groups. This section could be extended much further if you have time. For example, ask students to create a questionnaire about likes and dislikes. Students then have to interview ten people and present their findings to the rest of the class at a later date.

Photocopy and cut out the *Useful language* on page 78 to provide some extra support.

Vocabulary skill

Before you ask students to read the *Forming plurals* box, write some simple examples on the board, such as *brother, bus, activity*, etc. Briefly highlight that these rules only apply to countable nouns, and uncountable nouns do not take a plural form. A common example is *information*. Explain how the plural is made by adding *piece → pieces of information*. Then, ask students to read the box. Address any questions that they may have.

1   Do the first word together as a class. When the students have finished, check the answers together and practice the pronunciation of the words.

ANSWERS	
1 boy	5 baby
2 tooth	6 knife
3 watch	7 country
4 person	8 woman

2   Ask students to work individually to do exercise 2. Then check the answers and the pronunciation with the class.

ANSWERS	
1 parents	5 cities
2 potatoes	6 men
3 dishes	7 lives
4 children	8 days

EXTENSION ACTIVITY

Give students some sentences with noun form errors to correct. For example:

1 *My cousin has two babys.* (babies)

2 *There are 27 countrys in the European Union.* (countries)

3 *My boss is a women.* (woman)

4 *My parentes are teachers.* (parents)

3   Ask students to find the words in the puzzle. Explain that the words may go across or down the grid.

ANSWERS

F	A	M	I	L	I	E	S	Y
E	W	E	S	A	Y	R	I	N
E	U	N	T	J	M	H	R	S
T	O	S	W	E	H	E	P	I
O	C	H	I	L	D	R	E	N
C	L	I	V	E	S	O	O	G
B	O	X	E	S	G	E	P	E
S	D	I	S	H	E	S	L	R
A	B	G	C	I	T	I	E	S

4   As students are doing this task, circulate and monitor their pronunciation of individual letters. This activity could be done competitively as a whole class or in small groups.

SPEAKING   Interviewing a classmate

Exam tip

The types of questions in this section are similar to part 1 of the speaking test in the International English Language Testing System (IELTS). If you have students in your class who plan to take an IELTS Test in the future, you could explain the basic structure of the test and the relevance of this section to part 1. Part 1 is a set of three questions related to general topics, such as family, hobbies, work, studies, etc. There are some examples on the official IELTS website (www.ielts.org).

Pronunciation skill

You could ask students to practice reading aloud some of the words from the *Vocabulary skill* section. As students read out the words, write them on the board and group them by the pronunciation of the ending. Ask students to think about why you have grouped them that way. They might notice the pattern; if not, refer them to the *Plural endings* box.

1   Check that students are clear about which sound they are listening for in each column. Ask students to work in pairs and read aloud to each other.

ANSWERS
See audio script 1.06.

2   After the students have listened to the audio and checked their answers, ask them to put three or four of the words into sentences. For example: *I have two classes in the morning.*

AUDIO SCRIPT	1.06	
/s/	/z/	/ɪz/
apps	bags	boxes
desks	fans	classes
parents	kinds	edges
	lives	matches
	teachers	

3   Ask students to read the conversation and underline all of the plural nouns. Ask students to decide what they think the pronunciation of the plural nouns is, then listen to the audio and check.

AUDIO SCRIPT 1.07

A: What are your interests, Lisa?

B: I read a lot on weekends. I like novels.

A: I have three boxes of old books. Do you want them?

B: Sure. Thank you!

A: I only read magazines.

B: What kinds?

A: I like to read about sports, movies, and video games.

ANSWERS

A: What are your interest/s/, Lisa?

B: I read a lot on weekend/z/. I like novel/z/.

A: I have three box/ɪz/ of old book/s/. Do you want them?

B: Sure. Thank you!

A: I only read magazine/z/.

B: What kind/z/?

A: I like to read about sport/s/, movie/z/, and video game/z/.

4 Ask students to practice the conversation in exercise 3. Choose a pair to model the conversation for the class.

EXTENSION ACTIVITY

Ask students to adapt and change the conversation so that it matches their interests. Choose one or two pairs to practice their conversation in front of the class.

Grammar

As this is the first grammar section in the book, you might want to review the parts of a sentence by writing a very simple sentence on the board, and then asking students to identify the subject, verb, and object of the sentence.

With the verb *be*, you could write *am*, *is*, and *are* on the board and ask students if they know when to use each of them. Elicit an example sentence for each. Then ask students to read the *Grammar* box.

1 Ask students to complete the task individually.

ANSWERS

1 Are   2 Am   3 Is   4 Is   5 Are

2 After students have asked and answered the questions, ask one pair to model their questions for the class.

EXTENSION ACTIVITY

You could further test students' understanding by writing five or six sentences for students to correct on the board. For example, write: *Is apples your favorite fruit? Is all our classmates from the same country? Am you Saudi? Are reading your favorite hobby?*

3 Before asking students to write the correct questions, you could first give an example using a question in a previous section of this unit. For example, write on the board: *What be your favorite color?*

ANSWERS

1 Where are you from?
2 What is your family name?
3 What day is today?
4 Who is your best friend?

4 Ask students to practice asking and answering the questions in exercise 3 with a partner.

EXTENSION ACTIVITY

These exercises could be extended to recycle vocabulary and grammar from other sections of the unit; thus, making the interview section more thorough.

Speaking skill

Before asking students to read the *Asking for repetition* box, you could exemplify the concept with a small task. Tell students you are going to ask them to write down a name, address, and phone number. Say each detail individually but do so in a very fast way that makes it very difficult for students to complete. When you get to the end, check how many students have managed to write all of the details down—probably not many. Then ask students what they can say if they need something repeated. Elicit answers or refer students to the box if they cannot think of anything.

1 Before playing the audio, ask students to guess what might be said in each of the blanks.

AUDIO SCRIPT 1.08

1

A: This app is called Monster Mix.

B: Can you repeat that?

A: This app is called Monster Mix.

2

C: I'm from Dayton, Ohio, in the United States.

D: What's your hometown again?

C: Dayton.

3

A: The show starts at 5:45.

B: Can you please say that again?

A: The show starts at 5:45.

4

C: My full name is Sandra Renee Richards.

D: What's your middle name again?

C: Renee.

ANSWERS
1 repeat that
2 your hometown again
3 please say that again
4 your middle name again

2 Ask students to ask and answer the questions with a partner. As an extension, you could ask different students to answer the questions directly to you as a model for the class to analyze.

SPEAKING TASK

Model this first task with an example on the board, and then do two more as a whole class before having students work in pairs.

ANSWERS
1 What is your full name? Amina Omara
2 Do you have a nickname? no
3 Where are you from? Tripoli, Libya
4 What is your favorite color? red
5 Do you like sports? yes
6 What are your favorite sports? basketball and tennis
7 Do you like comic books? yes
8 What is your favorite video game? Final Fantasy

Brainstorm and plan

This might be the first time students have tried to brainstorm in English, so it might work better to model the first interview stages on the board before breaking students up into smaller groups.

Ask students to select four to six of the questions they think are the most interesting. Have them check their use of plurals and the verb *be*. This might be better done in pairs. Although it is good to encourage self-editing, it can be challenging at this level.

Speak and share

As students complete this stage, listen and make notes of any errors with the pronunciation of the verb *be* and plural endings. When students have finished their interviews, write any problem sentences on the board and practice the pronunciation together.

After students have introduced their partners in groups, choose one group to model their conversation to the whole class. During this stage, monitor and take language notes. Use the photocopiable *Unit assignment checklist* on page 88 to assess the students' speaking.

STUDY SKILLS Understanding classroom language

The concept of independent learning and taking responsibility for one's own progress might be new for some students. This especially can be the case for students who are just about to start their academic career. You might want to introduce the concept in general before starting this task. You could ask students what they expect the main differences between high school and university to be.

You could then lead a discussion about the role of the students and the teacher in terms of taking responsibility for learning and classroom interaction. This is a chance for you to model how you would like students to ask questions and when.

Getting started

Before assigning the task, explain that it is important that students feel confident to ask for help when they need it. Some students can be embarrassed to ask for repetition as they think it will show that they are weak. However, explain that they are probably not the only ones who don't understand. Try to encourage students to ask for help whenever they need to.

ANSWERS
1 T   2 S   3 S   4 T   5 T   6 E
7 E   8 T   9 T   10 E   11 T   12 S

Scenario

Give the students time to read the scenario and make suggestions for Francisco. Help students with any problem words. Have a whole-class discussion to share ideas.

POSSIBLE ANSWER
Francisco understands and can respond to many questions in English. He refers to a list of classroom language. He also practices classroom language with a partner. However, he should try to respond in English even when his partner doesn't speak in English.

Consider it

After students have discussed the tips with a partner, open the discussion to the whole class. You may want to add a few of your own personal suggestions to encourage students to behave in the manner you would like.

Over to you

If students have difficulty with this task, you could do this as a whole class discussion instead.

UNIT 2 FAMILY

Listening	Listening for details
Vocabulary	Organizing words: diagrams
Grammar	Possessive adjectives
Speaking	Asking follow-up questions
Pronunciation	Syllables

Discussion point

Ask students to look at the picture on page 17 and suggest who the people in it might be. (The picture is of a traditional nomadic Kazakh family.) Then write on the board a set of family-related words with one of each "pair" missing. For example, write *father* _____, *sister* _____, *husband* _____, *daughter* _____, *grandfather* _____. If students find these sets quite easy, you could extend it to wider family members, such as *aunt, uncle, cousin,* or even *half sister, stepsister,* etc.

Ask students to discuss the questions with a partner, using the sentence frames to help them get started. After they have discussed the questions, ask one or two students to share their answers with the class.

EXTENSION ACTIVITY

You could then extend the discussions by doing a "Find someone who …" task. Students have to find someone in the class who has: more brothers than they do, fewer sisters than they do, more aunts than they do, etc. You might want to write a question on the board to help guide students, such as: *How many aunts do have you have? How many brothers do you have?* When completed, students could present to the class any interesting information, such as who has the most brothers, the biggest family, etc.

This is a good place to use the video resource *Around the dinner table,* as it gives some good ideas about the importance of family. It is located in the Video resources section of the digital component. Alternatively, remind the students about the video resource so they can do this at home.

Cultural awareness

Families differ significantly around the world. Depending on the different cultures you have in the classroom, this could be an interesting topic to pick up on, especially the concept of the extended family living together, or the idea of people living alone, which both tend to differ greatly between cultures. For example, according to Euromonitor International, 47% of Swedish people live alone, 31% of Japanese people live alone, 10% of Brazilians live alone, and 3% of Indians live alone. These might be interesting areas for discussion.

Vocabulary preview 1

1 Draw students' attention to the picture and note that each person has a name label. Give the first answer to the students as an example.

ANSWERS	
1 father	5 sister
2 son	6 daughter
3 wife	7 brother
4 mother	8 husband

2 Have students work in pairs to do the task. When the students have finished, ask them to write down the names of their own parents, and brothers and sisters. They can make true or false sentences and have a partner work out who the people are.

LISTENING 1 Tell me about your family

Before you listen

Have students work in pairs to describe the pictures. To extend and personalize this task, you could ask students to show each other any pictures they have of their family. Students can then explain who the people are to a partner.

Global listening

Background information

Completing questionnaires and being stopped for an interview in the street can be common in some countries; however, in others it might be very unusual. You might need to explain the concept before playing the audio.

Before playing the audio, ask students to guess who will be speaking for each picture. Then ask how this might change some of the vocabulary the person uses, e.g., *husband, wife, mother, father.* Play the audio, then check the answers as a class.

AUDIO SCRIPT 1.09

1

Int: Hello, excuse me.

M1: Yes.

Int: Do you have a minute?

M1: Um, sure.

Int: Great. What's your name?

M1: Kyle.

Int: I'm interviewing people about their family.

M1: Um, OK …

Int: How many people are in your family?

M1: In my family? Well, there's me, and my father and mother …

Int: And what do they do?

M1: Their jobs? My father's a police officer, and my mother's a teacher.

Int: Do you have any brothers and sisters?

M1: Yes. I have an older brother and a younger sister. My brother's a university student, and my sister's in elementary school.

Int: Are you a student, too?

M1: Yeah. I'm in middle school.

Int: Well, thank you very much, Kyle.

M1: You're welcome.

2

Int: Excuse me.

F1: Yes?

Int: I'm interviewing people about their families. Do you have a second?

F1: Sure, I guess so.

Int: Great. What's your name?

F1: My name is Andrea.

Int: Are you married?

F1: Yes. My husband's name is George.

Int: And do you have children?

F1: Yes, we do. We have three kids.

Int: How nice! Tell me about them.

F1: Well, we have two daughters, Emilia and Natalia. And one son, Jim.

Int: Are they all in school?

F1: My daughters are, but not Jim. My sister is with him now, so I need to get home.

Int: OK. Thank you for your time.

3

F2: I see you are interviewing people about families.

Int: Oh, um, yes.

F2: Do you want to hear about my family?

Int: Of course.

F2: My name is Laura. I'm 16. I'm a high school student.

Int: How many people are in your family?

F2: There are four people in my family. There are my parents, me, and my little sister. She's in elementary school. She's 11.

Int: What's your sister like?

F2: She's very smart for her age.

Int: Do you have any brothers?

F2: No, but I want one.

Int: OK. Well, thanks, Laura.

F2: That's it? No more questions?

Int: No, that's all.

ANSWERS
1 c   2 a   3 b

Close listening

Ask the students to read the *Listening for details* box. Then tell them to follow the three steps described in the box when they do exercise 1.

1   Before playing the audio again, you might need to check students understand the meaning of some words in the exercise, e.g., *smart* and *funny*.

ANSWERS
1 a   2 a   3 a   4 b   5 b   6 a

2   Have the students work individually to do the task, then ask them to share their answers with a partner. As an extra task, you could ask students to use the adjectives *older* and *younger* to describe their family again. You could also explain that some people will say they have a *big sister* or a *little sister*, and that these mean the same as an *older/ elder sister* and a *younger sister*.

ANSWERS
1 b, e   2 c, f   3 a, d

Over to you

Question 1 will have been covered to some extent already in previous tasks so should be considered more as a review. For question 2, write the four words from the *Think about* box on the board with three or four lines drawn from each to create small mind maps. Elicit the ways people can be different in each category with words such as *tall, blond, short, brown, soccer, tennis, computer games, intelligent, funny*, etc. Photocopy and cut out the *Useful language* on page 79 to provide some extra support.

Vocabulary preview 2

1   Depending on the students' knowledge, some of these words may have already come up earlier in the unit. Work through the first sentence with the class. Explain that *-in-law* can be added to other family words, but typically only *brother, sister, father*, and *mother*. Have the students do the exercise, then check their answers with a partner.

ANSWERS
1 d   2 a   3 c   4 b   5 f   6 g   7 h   8 e

2   Ask students to work with a partner to do the exercise. The first answer is given for the students. To extend this activity, you could get students to name someone in their family for each relative. They could then tell their partner a trait they have that is similar or different to that relative.

ANSWERS
1 your uncle   4 your grandmother
2 your aunt   5 your sister/sister-in-law
3 your niece   6 your cousin

LISTENING 2 All in the family

Before you listen

Background information
Typically, a circus in western Europe is a traveling company of performers that may include clowns, acrobats, trained animals, trapeze acts, musicians, tightrope walkers, jugglers, unicyclists, and other stunt-oriented artists. Older versions of circuses from Greek and Roman times would have included things such as staged battles and chariot races. You could find a video clip of a circus online to show students who are not familiar with the concept.

Refer students to the *Adjectives* box on page 20. Explain any unknown words and then check students' understanding by asking questions, such as: *What do you think is boring? What sports are dangerous? What food do you think is strange?* Then discuss the question as a class.

Global listening

1 Before playing the audio, you could ask students what personal experience they have of performing, e.g., school plays, dance recitals, etc.

AUDIO SCRIPT 1.10
The Hansen family is a normal family. There is Shane, the father, Alecia, the mother, and their three daughters: Olivia, Madison, and Ella. But do they have a normal life? Not really.

The Hansen family are circus performers. They entertain people all over the United States with an exciting 30-minute show. Both Shane and Alecia were performers as children with their own parents—Shane from age three and Alecia from age nine. It's a family tradition.

The Hansen family perform for ten months a year. They perform outdoors from June to September. In October and November, they perform indoors, at places like basketball games and on boats. They also perform indoors from March to May.

ANSWERS
people in the family, where they perform, their performance schedule

EXTENSION ACTIVITY
Ask students to describe their own schedule to a partner.

2 Before playing the second part of the audio, you could ask students to tell each other about their own free-time activities. Then ask them to guess what activities the Hansen family might do in their free time.

AUDIO SCRIPT 1.11
In December and January, they don't perform. They relax, and see their friends and family. Shane likes to

play football and golf. Alecia likes to ride her bicycle. The children love to play at the beach.

When they perform, they do *all* the work. They build the sets and make the costumes. Their costumes are blue and white. Alecia believes blue and white are happy colors. Many circus performers like wearing red, but Alecia thinks red is an angry color.

The family travel a lot. They drive 35,000 miles a year. They love to see different parts of the United States. Their life on the road is comfortable. They travel with a TV, video games, and an Internet connection.

The family love what they do and don't plan to stop. Who knows? Someday, maybe Shane and Alecia's grandchildren will continue the family tradition.

ANSWERS
their free-time activities, their costumes, life on the road

Close listening

1 Ask the class if they can remember the three close listening strategies in the *Listening for details* box on page 19. Brainstorm these on the board. Play the audio and ask students to use these strategies when they do the exercise.

AUDIO SCRIPT 1.12
The Hansen family is a normal family. There is Shane, the father, Alecia, the mother, and their three daughters: Olivia, Madison, and Ella. But do they have a normal life? Not really.

The Hansen family are circus performers. They entertain people all over the United States with an exciting 30-minute show. Both Shane and Alecia were performers as children with their own parents—Shane from age three and Alecia from age nine. It's a family tradition.

The Hansen family perform for ten months a year. They perform outdoors from June to September. In October and November, they perform indoors, at places like basketball games and on boats. They also perform indoors from March to May.

In December and January, they don't perform. They relax, and see their friends and family. Shane likes to play football and golf. Alecia likes to ride her bicycle. The children love to play at the beach.

When they perform, they do *all* the work. They build the sets and make the costumes. Their costumes are blue and white. Alecia believes blue and white are happy colors. Many circus performers like wearing red, but Alecia thinks red is an angry color.

The family travel a lot. They drive 35,000 miles a year. They love to see different parts of the United States. Their life on the road is comfortable. They travel with a TV, video games, and an Internet connection.

The family love what they do and don't plan to stop. Who knows? Someday, maybe Shane and Alecia's grandchildren will continue the family tradition.

ANSWERS

1 T	2 F	3 T	4 F	5 T	6 F	7 F	8 T

2 Ask students to close their books. Elicit the names of the 12 months of the year and then ask different students to spell them. Write the months on the board, dealing with any mistakes as they occur. Then drill the pronunciation of each. Play the audio and ask the students to complete the excerpt.

AUDIO SCRIPT   1.13
The Hansen family perform for ten months a year. They perform outdoors from June to September. In October and November, they perform indoors, at places like basketball games and on boats. They also perform indoors from March to May. In December and January, they don't perform. They relax, and see their friends and family.

ANSWERS
The Hansen family perform for ten months a year. They perform outside from June to September. In October and November, they perform indoors, at places like basketball games and on boats. They also perform indoors from March to May. In December and January, they don't perform. They relax, and see their friends and family.

Over to you

Ask students to discuss the questions with a partner. Refer them to the *Think about* box for ideas. You could then extend this by asking students what they would miss if they had to go away from home for a few months of the year.

Vocabulary skill

1 Ask students to read the *Organizing words: diagrams* box and explain that a Venn diagram is a way of recording vocabulary. Learning words in groups helps make connections. Moreover, using a diagram to show these groupings is good for visual learners. As a guide, ask students where they would put the word *aunt* and the word *grandparent*.

ANSWERS

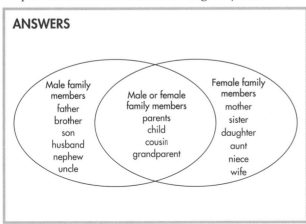

2 Before having students complete the family tree, brainstorm adjectives to describe people on the board. Make sure students have around eight to ten adjectives that they can then use to label the people in the family tree.

ANSWERS

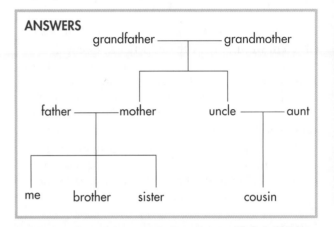

EXTENSION ACTIVITY

Ask students to draw their own family tree, then exchange their tree with a partner. Their partner should write three or four sentences describing the family tree.

SPEAKING Presenting your family tree

Grammar

As a lead-in, you could use items around the classroom to model each of the different possessive adjectives. Pick up an item such as a pen and say aloud: *This is her pen.* Make sure that each time, you stress the possessive adjectives. Do this for three of the possessive adjectives before asking the students which words you stressed. Repeat the sentences if necessary and then write the three possessive adjectives on the board. Ask students if they know any other possessive adjectives in English. Then ask students to read the *Grammar* box.

1 Copy the first sentence on the board. Read aloud both options and ask a student which one is correct. Clarify the genders of niece/nephew if there is any confusion.

ANSWERS

1 Her	2 Their	3 My	4 Our
5 Your	6 Its	7 his	

2 For weaker students, you might want to give a limited number of options for each blank. When the students have finished, ask them to read the conversation aloud with a partner.

ANSWERS

1 Its	4 our	7 her	10 my
2 my	5 your	8 my/our	11 your
3 my	6 my/our	9 their	12 my

3 Have students work in groups to describe members of their family or friends. You might want to have students focus on using possessive adjectives accurately.

Pronunciation skill

Write the word *syllable* on the board as well as three different words: one with one syllable, one with two, and one with three syllables. Draw vertical lines between each syllable to highlight how the word is broken down. Read the words aloud and ask the class to repeat them. Have students read the *Syllables* box, and then drill the pronunciation of the examples.

1 Write three more words on the board and ask students how many syllables each one has. Then ask students to do the exercise individually, then listen and check their answers.

AUDIO SCRIPT 1.14
1 uncle, 2, un-cle
2 wife's, 1, wife's
3 husband, 2, hus-band
4 nieces, 2, nie-ces
5 colleges, 3, col-le-ges
6 initials, 3, i-ni-tials
7 questions, 2, ques-tions
8 actor, 2, ac-tor
9 blue, 1, blue
10 grandparent, 3, grand-pa(r)-rent
11 school, 1, school
12 cousin, 2, cou-sin

ANSWERS

1	2; un/cle	7	2; ques/tions
2	1; wife's	8	2; ac/tor
3	2; hus/band	9	1; blue
4	2; nie/ces	10	3; grand/pa/rent
5	3; col/le/ges	11	1; school
6	3; i/ni/tials	12	2; cou/sin

---

2 After they have practiced the words in exercise 1, ask students to add more words with varying numbers of syllables and to practice those with their partner.

Speaking skill

Background information
One of the main reasons students can struggle to have a fluent conversation in a second language is because it takes some time to transfer "normal" conversational behavior over to another language. One such area for lower level students is the concept of asking follow-up questions. They are often so worried about understanding another speaker that they do not start to plan their response.

Before asking students to read the *Asking follow-up questions* box, you could exemplify the concept. Ask one student questions such as: *Who do you live with?* followed by: *Is your house/apartment large?* Now write another topic on the board, such as *family* or *friends,* and ask students to ask and answer questions on the topics with each other.

1 Before playing the audio, ask students to read the questions and have them guess with a partner what the statement said before the question might have been. You might need to give the first one as an example.

AUDIO SCRIPT 1.15
1 My brother is a student.
2 There are six people in my family.
3 My sister is married.
4 My aunt's name is Celia.
5 My brother's favorite class is Literature.
6 Our new teacher is Mr. Chang.
7 My grandparents live in Los Angeles.
8 My cousin studies Engineering.

ANSWERS
1 What's his major?
2 Do you live with your parents?
3 What's her name?
4 What's she like?
5 What's his favorite book?
6 Where is he from?
7 How often do you see them?
8 Where does your cousin go to school?

---

2 Play the audio and check the answers together as a class. As a follow up, ask students to practice the short conversations in pairs.

AUDIO SCRIPT 1.16
1
My brother is a student.
What's his major?
2
There are six people in my family.
Do you live with your parents?
3
My sister is married.
What's her name?
4
My aunt's name is Celia.
What's she like?
5
My brother's favorite class is Literature.
What's his favorite book?
6
Our new teacher is Mr. Chang.
Where is he from?

7

My grandparents live in Los Angeles.

How often do you see them?

8

My cousin studies Engineering.

Where does your cousin go to school?

3 Ask students to do the exercise in groups, then write the statements from exercise 2 on the board. Ask the students to make the statements true for themselves and to work in pairs to ask a follow-up question.

SPEAKING TASK

If you have done some of the *Extension activities* before, students may have tried something similar already. However, this task raises the challenge by actually setting this as a mini-presentation task.

1 Ask one student to read the text aloud. When the students have completed the activity, check the answers together and drill any problem words.

ANSWERS

My name is Kevin. I have a large family. I live with my parents. My father is an engineer. His name is George. My mother is a nurse. Her name is Carol. I have two sisters. One is a university student. She's 21. Her name is Dana. Her major is European history. My older sister is Jennifer. She and her husband live near us. Their son is named Peter. I like my nephew a lot. He's very funny. My grandmother lives with us. She's my father's mother. She's seventy years old.

2 Ask students to work with a partner to think of follow-up questions, them ask them to write their questions on the board. This will help show the students the range of possibilities.

Brainstorm and plan

If you have students from cultures where extended families can be large, you might want to suggest that students just focus on their immediate nuclear family when they draw their family tree.

Tell students that they do not have to talk about everyone in their family tree, but in total they should have at least ten things to say about their family.

Speak and share

Encourage students to peer correct and help each other, especially with some of the vocabulary to describe interests and personalities.

If you have the technology and the time, you could have students produce a more formal presentation. During this stage, monitor and take language notes. Use the photocopiable *Unit assignment checklist* on page 89 to assess the students' speaking.

STUDY SKILLS Working with others

Background information

Many university systems around the world encourage collaboration with others. Teamwork skills are seen as ones that are transferable to the workplace; they are also seen as key elements of the academic community. Practical degrees that require experimentation and fieldwork, such as the sciences, often require students to do experiments and research together. Also, subjects very closely related to professions, such as a number of business degrees, place a great emphasis on teamwork in assessments such as giving group presentations.

Getting started

Explain to students that it is important to feel comfortable working in groups and teams, as they are likely to have to do so both during their studies and in their careers. Have students discuss the questions and then share ideas on the board. You could extend this into a brainstorm of the advantages and disadvantages of teamwork.

Scenario

Give students time to read the scenario and make suggestions for Amina. Help students with any problem words. Have a whole-class discussion to share ideas.

POSSIBLE ANSWER

Amina likes to work with others and to listen to others while she is working. However, she doesn't contribute much to the discussion, and she prefers not to work with people who have very different ideas. In addition, her group doesn't collaborate with others.

Consider it

After students have discussed the tips with a partner, open the discussion to the whole class. You may want to add a few of your own suggestions to encourage students to behave in the manner you would like when working with others in class.

Over to you

Ask students to discuss the questions using the tips given in the *Consider it* section.

Extra research task

Ask students to use the Internet to research their degree subject (U.S. = major) or intended degree and to find out what expectations there are for group work. Is it something they might be assessed on?

UNIT 3 STUFF

Listening	Activating prior knowledge
Vocabulary	Identifying parts of speech in a dictionary
Grammar	Possessive pronouns
Pronunciation	Word stress
Speaking	Asking what something is called

Discussion point

Elicit what students can see in the picture on page 27. They might not know the word *snowglobe* at this level, so you might need to give some hints. Similarly, students might not have encountered the word *stuff* before. *Stuff* can be used to refer to many things without being specific, e.g., *I need to do my homework and stuff. I have too much stuff. I have too much stuff in my closet. Stuff* is generally an informal word. Ask students to discuss the questions with a partner, using the sentence frames to help them get started. Photocopy and cut out the *Useful language* on page 80 to provide some extra support. Ask what they can see in each snowglobe. You could also ask students what might be in a snowglobe of their city or country.

With question 2, try to get students to give reasons to support their opinions. In academic contexts, even at lower levels, it is important to always push students to explain and justify their answers, and to not allow one-word answers.

Have students refer to the *Things people collect* box for ideas when discussing question 3. Alternatively, if you or someone you know collects something, you could tell the students about the collection. If students show enthusiasm for this topic, you could encourage them to bring in a collection or pictures of their collection to show the class.

Background information

Collecting things became common across the world as people traveled further and experienced new cultures. Many original collections were of unusual or curious things that people found on their travels. There are specific words to refer to different types of collecting. For example, philately = the collecting of stamps; numismatics = the collecting of coins; lepidoptery = the collecting of (dead) butterflies.

Vocabulary preview 1

1 Before having students label the pictures, show them a selection of everyday items; either real objects, pictures, or flashcards. They could be the items in exercise 1 or other items. Elicit the names of the different items.

ANSWERS

1 i	2 a	3 k	4 g	5 c	6 d
7 j	8 f	9 b	10 e	11 l	12 h

2 To lead into this task, ask students to guess what their partner has in their bag. Ask students to do the task in groups.

LISTENING 1 Something special

Before you listen

1 Before asking students to fill in the chart, elicit from one or two students how they would feel if they lost an item from their bag. Choose a simple thing like a pen for one person and something more valuable or personal for the other person. Ask students to do the activity, then check their answers in pairs.

2 Ask students to discuss the question together and then share their ideas with the class. Write everyone's answers on the board to see what item the whole class would least like to lose. Pick up on any unusual ones for further discussion and ask the class why they think one or two items are the ones most people would not like to lose.

Background information

Listening is arguably the hardest thing anyone can do in a second language. In the classroom, recordings are slower, clearer, and have vocabulary and grammar that is appropriate for the level; however, the challenge is still high. It involves processing individual words, putting those words back together to create a proposition, and then using that to answer a question the students have just read or are reading simultaneously. Therefore, it is really important for students to activate any prior knowledge on a topic. This schemata-raising can really help students engage with and understand better the topic in question.

3 Before asking students to identify what they see in the pictures, have them read the *Activating prior knowledge* box.

ANSWERS

a a (baseball) cap
b a (cell/smart) phone
c a (black) (leather) wallet
d a stuffed animal/cat
e a watch

4 Ask students to work in pairs to do the task. Allow any answers that are possible and make sense.

Global listening

With stronger classes, encourage students to make notes of any other information they hear as they listen. Have them listen and number the pictures.

AUDIO SCRIPT   1.17

1

Rick: Hello. I'm Rick. Um, I want to show you this watch. It has a special meaning for me. It's an expensive watch, but that's not why it's special to me. It's my grandfather's watch. It's my only possession of his. It's about 50 years old. It doesn't work, but I wear it sometimes.

2

Penny: My name is Penny. I have something special, too. Let me introduce you to Allie. Yes, it's a cat. Isn't Allie cute? Now don't laugh. It's from my grandfather. He likes to give me stuffed animals. I also have a bird, a horse, and a fish. I keep them on my desk at home. It makes me happy when I look at them.

3

Victor: Hello everyone. My name is Victor. I have something to show you, too. You all have one, I think. Any guesses? No? OK, it's my cell phone. I always have it in my pocket or my book bag. I think it's really cool because it does a lot of interesting things. And I have all my favorite photos on it. Do you want to see them? I have … Oh! … hello?

4

Emiko: Hi. I'm Emiko. I am wearing something right now with a special meaning. It's my baseball cap. Isn't it great? I go to a lot of baseball games, and I wear it every game. I love all sports, such as basketball, soccer, and tennis, but baseball is my favorite. But strangely enough—I don't have a favorite team.

5

Terry: I'm Terry, and I have something special from Italy. Here it is—it's a black wallet. Nice, huh? This wallet is a gift from my e-pal in Rome. His name is Stefano. Now, let's look inside. I have my student card, my bus pass, but um … it doesn't have any money in it. Hmm, who wants to buy me lunch?

ANSWERS

1 e   2 d   3 b   4 a   5 c

Close listening

Before you play the audio again, ask students to read the sentences to themselves and try to predict the type of information they will hear. You could model the first two blanks by eliciting from the class that they are likely to hear an adjective for the first blank and a number in the second blank. When students have done this, ask them to compare with a partner. You may also want to ask students if they remember why each of the items pictured is special. Model the first one on the board and take as many different answers as possible from students. The wider the range the

better, as this will stimulate their discussion on the rest of the items.

ANSWERS

1 expensive; (about) 50	3 book bag; (really) cool
2 cat/animal; grandfather	4 game; sports
	5 Italy; money

Over to you

Depending on the class, this task could be extended into quite a long discussion. You could talk about when and where people like to shop, who people buy for, what things they buy on vacation, etc.

Vocabulary preview 2

1   Ask students to match the words with the meanings. After checking the answers, you could elicit what concept these things all have in common: *organization*. You could also ask students which of the nouns they use themselves and which of the adjectives they would use to describe themselves.

ANSWERS

1 c   2 d   3 b   4 a   5 h   6 e   7 f   8 g

---

2   When students have completed the sentences, you could ask them to discuss the goals with a partner and tell each other whether they would set any of the goals personally.

ANSWERS

1 organized	5 reminder
2 on time	6 messy
3 hurry	7 full
4 planner	8 folders

LISTENING 2 Get organized

This is a good place to use the video resource *Messy desk, messy mind*. It is located in the Video resources section of the digital component. Alternatively, remind the students about the video resource so they can do this at home.

Before you listen

1   Before having students check the statements, review adverbs of frequency by writing a scale on the board: *never, rarely, sometimes, often, usually, always.*

2   Ask the students to add up their scores and then compare them with a partner. Have students find someone with a very different score from their score. The organized person should try to give the disorganized person three pieces of advice using *You should …*

Global listening

Before playing the audio, make sure students are clear that there are seven tips but only three pictures.

> **AUDIO SCRIPT 1.18**
>
> Good morning, everyone. My name is Jackie Donaldson. I want to start with a question. How many of you are organized? Go on, raise your hands. Hmm, OK, not so many. College life can be difficult sometimes. I know you are very busy people. That's why I am here today: to share some tips, or ideas, to help you, as students, become more organized. OK?
>
> **Tip 1:** Plan your day. Think about your day the night before and prepare anything you need. Maybe you want to put a magazine in your bag because you have a doctor's appointment?
>
> **Tip 2:** Don't hurry. Going fast makes you forget things. Need 30 minutes to get ready in the morning? Get up 45 minutes early. The bus comes at 7:30? Plan to be at the bus stop at 7:20. Relax, go slowly, and don't hurry.
>
> **Tip 3:** Use just one planner. You don't need one planner for school activities and another planner for personal activities. It's easy to mix up things that way. Think about this proverb: A man with two watches doesn't know the correct time.
>
> **Tip 4:** Use your cell phone for reminders. Most cell phones have a reminder feature. Put important information into your phone and then set it to send you a 15-minute, 30-minute, or 60-minute reminder.
>
> **Tip 5:** Keep school supplies in your book bag. You never know when you need a pen, pencil, paper, eraser, stapler, or highlighter. Keep it all in your book bag. Don't remove these things at the end of the day. Leave them here. Have other supplies at your desk.
>
> **Tip 6:** Use colored notebooks. Have a different colored notebook for each class, such as green for English, blue for engineering, and red for history. Try to match them to the cover of the textbook to help you remember.
>
> **Tip 7:** Use colored highlighters. Different colors are also a good idea. For example, use yellow to highlight important information and green to highlight new words. This keeps your notes organized and easy to review.
>
> So there are your seven tips. What do you think? Are they helpful tips? Maybe you have ideas of your own.

> **ANSWERS**
> Picture a: Tip 4
> Picture b: Tip 7
> Picture c: Tip 2

Close listening

1 Ask students to listen again and complete the tips. Before playing the audio, give students a few minutes to complete any tips that they can from things they remember.

> **ANSWERS**
> 1 day   5 book bag
> 2 hurry   6 colored
> 3 planner   7 highlighters
> 4 reminders

2 Before playing the audio, tell students that they will need to match each extra piece of information to one of the tips in exercise 1.

> **AUDIO SCRIPT 1.19**
>
> a Put important information into your phone and then set it to send you a 15-minute, 30-minute, or 60-minute reminder.
> b For example, use yellow to highlight important information and green to highlight new words.
> c Think about your day the night before and prepare anything you need.
> d You never know when you need a pen, pencil, paper, eraser, stapler, or highlighter.
> e Going fast makes you forget things.
> f Try to match them to the cover of the textbook to help you remember.
> g You don't need one planner for school activities and another planner for personal activities.

> **ANSWERS**
> Sentence a: tip 4
> Sentence b: tip 7
> Sentence c: tip 1
> Sentence d: tip 5
> Sentence e: tip 2
> Sentence f: tip 6
> Sentence g: tip 3

Over to you

Ask students to discuss the questions in pairs or small groups, then elicit any other ideas and write them on the board. Ask students in pairs to create a list of the top three tips using both ideas from the book and from the board. When you have done this, ask students to compare their suggestions with the *Ways to be organized* box.

Vocabulary skill

Ask students to tell a partner what they do when they do not know the meaning of a word. Find out how many students use a print dictionary, how many use an online one, and how many have an app or a CD-ROM. Encourage students to share advice on the best dictionaries that they have used and why they like them. Note that *Using a learner's dictionary* features later on page 56 of the Student's Book as a *Study skills* activity.

Write the sentence below on the board and ask
students to label the part of speech for each word:

Elicit the word *adjective* from students, perhaps by
using an unfinished sentence frame such as: *Happy,
mad, bad, lovely, clear, messy, favorite are ...?* You could
use a similar framework to elicit the words *noun* and
verb, for example. Ask students to read the *Identifying
parts of speech in a dictionary* box. Then ask them to
look at the dictionary entry for the word *pet*.

1 Ask students to identify the underlined words in
   the sentences, then have them underline one more
   word in each sentence. Ask them to work with a
   partner. Their partner should try to name the part
   of speech for the additional underlined words. You
   may have to solve any disagreements.

ANSWERS
1 organized = adj.; late = adj.; hurry = v.
2 sometimes = adv.; into = prep.; reminder = n.
3 messy = adj.; I = pron.; on = prep.
4 get = v.; full = adj.; important = adj.

2 Ask students to do this exercise individually and
   then check the answers on the board together. Ask
   students if they know any other words with two
   meanings and get them to explain the difference
   in meaning.

ANSWERS

		Part of speech	Definition
1	She's in a terrible <u>state</u>.	noun	a condition
2	Please <u>state</u> your name.	verb	to say clearly
3	Let's <u>head</u> to class	verb	to go
4	My <u>head</u> hurts.	noun	the top of the body
5	It's <u>past</u> your bedtime.	adverb	after
6	Forget the <u>past</u>.	noun	the time before now

SPEAKING Talking about everyday items

Exam tip

Describing everyday objects, people, and places is a
common theme in many oral tests. This should be the
easiest subject matter to practice speaking about, since
these resources are all around the students. Students
should be encouraged to think in English about what

they can see around them. For example, while
traveling to class on the bus, students can silently
describe what they can see out of the bus window.

Grammar

Have students close their books, then elicit the
possessive pronouns and write them on the board.
Give the first one as an example. When you have done
this, ask students to read the *Grammar* box, and then
elicit an example sentence for each of the possessive
pronouns.

1 Before playing the audio to check answers, have
   students compare their answers with a partner.

AUDIO SCRIPT   1.20

1

Mike: Excuse me, Paul. Is this book yours?

Paul: No, it's not mine. My book is in my book bag.
Maybe it's Kevin's.

Mike: No, it's not his. His book is on his desk.

Danny: I think that book is mine. Let's see ... yes, my
initials "D.S." are here.

2

Lisa: Whose colored pens are these?

Klara: Yumiko and Paula like to draw. Maybe they are
theirs.

Lisa: Yumiko, are these pens yours and Paula's?

Yumiko: Oh, there they are! Yes, they're ours. Thanks!

ANSWERS
1 yours   5 theirs
2 mine   6 yours
3 his   7 ours
4 mine

2 Monitor as students do this task and drill any
   problematic sentences. Choose two groups to
   model the conversations for the rest of the class.

3 Ask students to practice this task as the book
   suggests. When they have done this, ask students
   to create a longer conversation using the ones in
   exercise 1 as a model. Choose one or two pairs to
   model their conversations for the class.

Pronunciation skill

Choose two words to highlight different stress
patterns such as *history* and *understand*. Drill students
on the correct pronunciation and then refer them to
the *Word stress* box.

1 Underline the stress on the first two words as
   examples for the class and then have students work
   together in pairs. Encourage students to read the
   words aloud as they do this task.

ANSWERS
1 feature
2 review
3 engineer
4 supplies
5 reminder
6 highlight
7 organized
8 stapler
9 expensive

2 After playing the audio, have students practice the words in pairs. Check and drill the words as a class.

AUDIO SCRIPT 1.21
1 feature
2 review
3 engineer
4 supplies
5 reminder
6 highlight
7 organized
8 stapler
9 expensive

Speaking skill

Before asking students to read the *Asking what something is called* box, you could exemplify the concept by writing some of the sentences from the box on the board with individual words missing. Then point to an object in the classroom and try to elicit the missing words from students. For example, write: *What's _____ called? What's the _____ for that in English? How do you _____ it in _____?*

You may need to make sure students are clear on the difference in use of *this* and *that.* Generally speaking, we use *this* when the item is physically nearer the speaker and *that* when it is further away from the speaker.

You could then write the phrases related to spelling on the board and repeat the same task.

How do you spell _____? Can you please _____ it?

1 Give students a few minutes to read the conversation beginnings. Ask students to guess any of the missing phrases before playing the audio. When students have completed the phrases, you could ask them to practice the conversations with a partner.

AUDIO SCRIPT 1.22
1
A: This necklace is my grandmother's. Isn't the stone pretty?
B: Yeah, it is. What's it called?
2
A: Do you like my new stuffed animal?
B: I do. How do you say that in English?
3
A: This hat is interesting.
B: It sure is. What's the word for it in English?

ANSWERS
1 What's it called?
2 How do you say that in English?
3 What's the word for it in English?

2 Before playing the audio, ask students to look at the three pictures and elicit what they are.

AUDIO SCRIPT 1.23
1
A: This necklace is my grandmother's. Isn't the stone pretty?
B: Yeah, it is. What's it called?
A: It's an opal.
B: Opal? How do you spell that?
A: O-P-A-L.
2
A: Do you like my new stuffed animal?
B: I do. How do you say that in English?
A: Hedgehog.
B: Hedgehog? Can you spell it?
A: Sure, it's H-E-D-G-E-H-O-G. It's cute, isn't it?
3
A: This hat is interesting.
B: It sure is. What's the word for it in English?
A: Beret, the stress is on the second syllable.
C: And how do you spell *beret*?
A: B-E-R-E-T. The *t* is silent.

ANSWERS
1 an opal (necklace)
2 a (stuffed) hedgehog
3 a beret

3 Ask students to look at the pictures in *Vocabulary preview 1* on page 28 and work with a partner to take turns asking about them. You could extend this task further with items in the classroom.

SPEAKING TASK

Model the task with an example on the board, and then do two more examples as a whole class. Alternatively, you could write or project the text on the board with some of the pronouns missing for students to complete. For example:

I have a special item. It's a statue of a cat. It's from Japan. It's from _____ parents' trip there. It's called *maneki neko* in Japanese. You see _____ in front of restaurants, banks, and offices. I believe they welcome people. I think _____ are good for business. My sister has one, too. I keep _____ in my bedroom, and she keeps _____ in _____ office at work. I think it's really cute!

ANSWERS

I have a special item. It's a statue of a cat. It's from Japan. It's from my parents' trip there. It's called *maneki neko* in Japanese. You see them in front of restaurants, banks, and offices. I believe they welcome people. I think they are good for business. My sister has one, too. I keep mine in my bedroom, and she keeps hers in her office at work. I think it's really cute!

Brainstorm

1 To exemplify this activity, you could take into class something that is special to you. Alternatively, you could display your special item as a picture or sketch on a piece of paper. It could be something that you could pretend to own, such as an antique vase. As students are doing this task, you might need to help them with vocabulary for their items. When everyone has three items written down, you could write them on the board and teach the words to the class, especially any words you think are useful or transferable for many students.

2 Encourage students to write answers to the three questions for each item. Also, encourage them to write down anything else interesting about the items.

Plan

Have students decide which special thing they think the class would like to find out about. If they are not sure, they could ask a partner which one they would like to know more about.

Speak and share

Ask students to tell their partner about their favorite thing. As an alternative, students could work in larger groups or with someone they did not do the planning stages with.

The *Share* task could be done informally from the desks, or you could encourage students to come to the front of the room so they get used to speaking in front of others. During this stage, monitor and take language notes. Use the photocopiable *Unit assignment checklist* on page 90 to assess the students' speaking.

STUDY SKILLS Creating a vocabulary notebook

Background information

Students are often very aware of the importance of learning grammar and vocabulary, and they are the things they often consider the most important to learn. However, not all students are effective at learning vocabulary. Many simply make a note of any new words in their notebooks with a first language translation next to it. At best, this may help with their passive understanding when reading, but it will make it difficult for students to use the words actively. This is a chance to instill some good learning strategies in students while they are still at a relatively low level.

Getting started

When students have discussed the questions with a partner, have them share their ideas with the class. If students are lacking in inspiration, you could give them a few ideas, such as:

Vocabulary cards—including a wide range of information such as pronunciation, an example sentence, the word family, common collocations

Vocabulary maps—on topics of related words, for example, words all related to the classroom

Scenario

Give students time to read the scenario and make suggestions for Ana. Help students with any problem words. Have a whole-class discussion to share ideas.

POSSIBLE ANSWER

Adding and removing pages can be good as you can get rid of pages with words you now know. However, it is unlikely that a student will know all words on one page at the same time, so cards with individual words on might be better. Topics are a good way to organize words. Collocations usually help students improve their vocabulary more rapidly. Translations are less likely to help Ana learn words than writing definitions, as it requires less mental effort. The lack of example sentences means Ana could struggle to move from a passive understanding to an active use.

Consider it

Ask students to discuss the ways to organize new words with a partner. You could tell students to try to rank the ideas from the best to the worst. If you do this, you might need to give them a sentence frame, e.g., *X is better because . . .*

Over to you

Ask students to try to use the different ways to organize new words suggested in the *Consider it* section when they decide how to organize the words.

Extra research task

Have students choose two or three of the ways to organize new words to try out in the next week. In the following class, ask students to tell their partner which method they found the most useful and why.

Money

Listening	Listening for numbers
Vocabulary	Using synonyms
Grammar	Demonstrative pronouns
Pronunciation	Intonation in questions
Speaking	Talking about prices

Discussion point

The picture on page 37 shows customers in a department store. Direct students' attention to the *Places to shop* box to help them with question 1. Encourage students to use some of this vocabulary rather than simply naming a store or a mall. You may want to give them a sentence frame to help, e.g., *I like to shop at … It's a …*

Ask students to say when they look carefully at prices, if at all. It is likely that they will consider the price when buying certain things such as clothes, but probably not when buying items such as snacks and drinks.

EXTENSION ACTIVITY

Have students talk about their favorite things to buy, how often they buy them, etc. by doing a "Find someone who …" activity. Some questions and follow up questions you could use are:

Find someone who …

… goes shopping every weekend.	Where do they go?
… thinks shopping is a hobby.	What other hobbies do they do?
… buys clothes every week.	What do they buy?
… hates shopping.	How do they get new things?
… shops more online than at real stores.	Why do they do this?

This is a good place to use the video resource *At the shops*. It is located in the Video resources section of the digital component. Alternatively, remind the students about the video resource so they can do this at home.

Vocabulary preview 1

1 Before students do the exercise, brainstorm what can be bought in each section of a department store by writing the eight sections on the board and eliciting ideas.

Cultural awareness

You might want to explain some of the differences between British English and American English for some items found in department stores.

British English	American English
handbag	purse
pants/knickers	underpants/panties
purse	wallet
tie	necktie
trousers	pants
vest	undershirt
waistcoat	vest

ANSWERS			
1 b	3 c	5 b	7 b
2 c	4 a	6 c	8 a

2 Ask students to tell their partner about their favorite department store. Then have them discuss the questions.

LISTENING 1 Can I help you?

Before you listen

Write two phrases on the board that could be said by a customer and two that could be said by a salesclerk. Then elicit who would say these phrases. For example, write: *Here's your change. Where's the men's clothing? What time do you close? Do you need help packing your bag?* Then ask students to decide who says each sentence.

As an extension, ask students to work with a partner to think of possible answers to any of the questions.

ANSWERS
S Can I help you?
S What size?
E Thank you.
C How much is it?
E Here you are.
S It looks nice on you.
S Cash or charge?
C Do you have it in black?
C Where is the fitting room?

Global listening

Ask students to close their books. Review the different sections of a department store again. Then have students listen and complete the chart.

AUDIO SCRIPT 1.24

1

Salesclerk: Can I help you?

Customer: Yes, where can I buy perfume?

Salesclerk: That's in the cosmetics section.

Customer: And where is that?

Salesclerk: On the first floor, next to women's clothing.

Customer: OK. And where am I now?

Salesclerk: You are on the third floor, in fashion accessories.

Customer: I see. Thanks.

2

Salesclerk: Can I help you?

Customer: Yes, how much is this basketball?

Salesclerk: It's $15.

Customer: And this tennis racket?

Salesclerk: That's $34.

Customer: OK, great. And where do I pay?

Salesclerk: Just over here. I can help you. Cash or charge?

Customer: Cash.

Salesclerk: That's $49.

Customer: Here you are.

Salesclerk: Thank you.

3

Salesclerk: Excuse me, but we close in 15 minutes.

Customer: Oh?

Salesclerk: Yes, we close at six on Sunday.

Customer: All right. How much are these earrings?

Salesclerk: They're $18.

Customer: And this necklace?

Salesclerk: That's $14. It looks good on you.

Customer: Thank you. You have very nice jewelry here.

Salesclerk: Thank you. We have some bracelets over here.

Customer: Oh, that's OK. I think just the necklace today.

Salesclerk: OK. That's $14, please.

4

Salesclerk: Can I help you?

Customer: Oh, yes, thank you. Do you have this blouse in black?

Salesclerk: I think so. What size?

Customer: Ten.

Salesclerk: Yes, here you are. Is this for …?

Customer: It's for my wife. Her birthday is next week, on the fourth.

Salesclerk: It's very nice. Is there anything else?

Customer: Um, yeah. Where's the electronics section? Is that on this floor?

Salesclerk: Electronics is on the second floor. But you need to pay for that blouse here, on this floor.

Customer: Oh, OK.

ANSWERS

	Section	What they are shopping for
1	fashion accessories	perfume
2	sporting goods	basketball, tennis racket
3	jewelry	necklace/jewelry
4	women's clothing	black blouse / gift for wife (and electronics)

Close listening

Write a selection of cardinal and ordinal numbers on the board, for example, *three, third, fifth, seven, one, first.* Then ask the students to put the numbers into two groups. Next, write *quantities, times, sizes, prices, dates,* and *the order of things in a sequence.* Elicit which ones use cardinal numbers and which use ordinal numbers. Ask students to read the *Listening for numbers* box. When they have finished, have them read the sentences with blanks and guess whether they will need an ordinal or cardinal number for each blank. Then play the audio for the students to complete the sentences.

ANSWERS
1 first	3 15	5 six	7 ten
2 third	4 34	6 18	8 second

Exam tip

The type of listening done here is similar to IELTS listening type 1 task, in which students have to pick out factual information such as numbers and names. If you have students preparing for the IELTS Test, you could create some additional sentences that require the students to identify words as well. For example:

Extract 1: The cosmetics section is on _____. (the third floor)

Extract 2: The customer wants to pay _____. (with cash)

Extract 3: The customer buys a _____. (necklace)

Extract 4: The _____ is on the second floor. (electronics section)

Over to you

Ask the students to discuss the questions in pairs or as a group. Then ask a couple of pairs or groups to report back their partner's or group's answers.

Vocabulary preview 2

1   Before asking students to complete the advertisement, make sure they understand the meaning of the words in the box. When the students have finished, check the answers with the class.

Money

ANSWERS

1	on sale	5	purchase
2	bargain	6	exchange
3	tag	7	receipt
4	discount	8	refund

2 Remind students of the adverbs of frequency and their different strengths. Write *never, seldom, sometimes, often, always* on the board in the wrong order and ask students to put them into the correct order from least to most frequent. Then have them discuss the questions with a partner.

Cultural awareness

In some countries, it can be very common to bargain for goods. In others, such as the U.K., people tend to bargain less. Trying to bargain in these countries can lead to embarrassment or awkwardness for all involved.

EXTENSION ACTIVITY

Ask students to discuss the idea of bargaining and receiving a discount. Set these questions for pairs to discuss:

Is it normal to bargain in your country?

How much discount do you ask for?

Do store owners always expect you to bargain?

Is there anything you would not bargain for?

LISTENING 2 Weekend sales

Before you listen

Give students a few minutes to describe where they buy the items in the pictures. Then have them report back to the whole class.

Cultural awareness

Students might know two of the items by their British English name. Write *trainers* and *football* on the board, and ask students which items they are in the pictures. *Trainers* are *sneakers* and a *football* is a *soccer ball* in American English.

Global listening

Give students a few minutes to read through the options; make sure students understand that they should choose only one option. Then play the audio.

AUDIO SCRIPT 1.25

1 Pixie's Pink Tag Sale

Come on down to Pixie's this Saturday and Sunday for our Pink Tag Sale. Pixie's sells all kinds of fabulous jewelry and fashion accessories, so shop for that special gift for that special someone. Find bargains on necklaces, belts, and scarves. They're all on sale now. Just look for an item with a pink tag and check the discount. Save 10%, 15%, or even 20%! Hurry for the best selection. There are no refunds or exchanges. All sales are final.

2 Electronics City Super Sale

Join us Friday night at Electric City for the start of our Super Sale. From Friday at ten o'clock until Sunday night at six o'clock, find all kinds of amazing discounts. Cell phones, cameras, TVs, computers—it's all here at Electric City. The first one hundred people to purchase items receive a 30% discount. The second one hundred people to purchase items receive a 20% discount. The third one hundred people to purchase items receive a 10% discount. Get in line early for the best bargains!

3 Madison's 24-Hour Sale

Head to Madison's this weekend. For 24 hours only, from ten a.m. Saturday to ten a.m. Sunday, everything at Madison's is on sale. That's right! We're open all night Saturday, so stop by anytime. Find bargains on clothing, shoes, and sports equipment. Bring in an old pair of sneakers and receive $20 off a new pair. Find us on the third floor of the Mega Mall.

4 Frank's Discounts Fun Sale!

Want to save money? Want to save BIG money? Then come to Frank's Discounts this weekend for our second Fun Sale of the year. Need something for the living room? Find tables for $39, lamps for $19, or chairs for $49. Or do you need something for the bedroom? We have beds for $129 and dressers for $79. Find amazing discounts at Frank's! We're open from nine a.m. to six p.m. Saturday and Sunday.

ANSWERS

1 jewelry and fashion accessories
2 electronics
3 sports equipment and clothing
4 furniture

Close listening

Have students practice reading the numbers in the sentences aloud. Do this once as a whole class and then ask students to practice in pairs. Then play the audio again for students to complete the task.

ANSWERS

1 a	3 b	5 a	7 a
2 a	4 b	6 b	8 a

Over to you

Draw students' attention to the *Places to find ads* box. Most items should be familiar to students, but as an additional task you could ask students to talk about which newspapers or magazines they read, what kinds of unwanted text messages they receive on their cell phones, which social networking sites they use, what TV shows they watch, and what websites they use regularly. Then ask them to discuss the questions in groups.

Vocabulary skill

Write the following adjectives on the board:

beautiful	*ugly*	*pretty*
loud	*quiet*	*noisy*

Elicit which one word in each set of three has a different meaning. Explain that the other pairs of words are synonyms and then ask students to read the *Using synonyms* box.

1 Have students work with a partner to match the synonyms. When they have finished, ask students to write four example sentences using two pairs of synonyms from the exercise.

> **ANSWERS**
> 1 difficult 3 large 5 similar
> 2 happy 4 near 6 fast

2 Before students do the matching task, ask them to read the sentences, and identify which of the bold words is a noun and which is a verb.

> **ANSWERS**
> 1 kids 5 carpet 9 speak
> 2 shop 6 couch 10 begin
> 3 present 7 get 11 choose
> 4 cab 8 end 12 purchase

3 When students have completed this task, ask different students to give you the sentence they made with one of the words. Write the sentences on the board and monitor any pronunciation problems.

4 After students have finished making lists of words and synonyms, give them another set of words from an earlier unit and ask them if they can think of any synonyms.

EXTENSION ACTIVITY

Write the following questions on the board. Ask students to complete them using words from exercises 1 and 2.

1 What subjects do you think are _____?
2 What interesting places are _____ your university?
3 Are you _____ or different to your parents?
4 What _____ did you get for your birthday?
5 What _____ do you shop in for clothes?
6 How often do you _____ music?

(Answers: 1 hard/difficult 2 near 3 similar 4 gifts 5 stores/shops 6 buy/purchase)

When students have completed the questions, ask them to discuss their answers in pairs.

SPEAKING Role-playing a shopping situation

Grammar

Introduce this activity by placing four sets of pens on a table. Place one pen near you, a group of pens near you, a single pen further away, and a group of pens further away. Write these phrases on the board twice:

_____ *pen*, _____ *pens*

Elicit *this*, *that*, *these*, and *those*. Then ask students to read the *Grammar* box. Make sure students are clear that the structure can also be used without a noun, and model an example if necessary.

1 Give students time to complete the sentences individually. Then ask students to compare their answers with a partner and practice the short conversations.

> **ANSWERS**
> 1 What's that?
>   It's a necktie.
> 2 What are these?
>   They're earrings.
> 3 What are those?
>   They're sneakers.
> 4 What's this?
>   It's a tennis racket.

2 Give students a few minutes to check the correct sentences and correct the incorrect sentences. Before checking the answers, tell students that two are correct and four are incorrect. If students have a different number, then they should check them again before you check as a class.

ANSWERS

1 ✓
2 These shoes hurt my feet. I need to sit down.
3 Listen to this podcast. Do you like it?
4 ✓
5 Those children in the other apartment are noisy!
6 Please put the books here. This is my desk.

3 Depending on your classroom, you might need to take a few items into the room to make this task work. Ask students to work in groups to ask and answer questions.

Pronunciation skill

Say the sentences from the *Intonation in questions* box and elicit if students noticed the intonation. Exaggerate the rising and falling pattern if necessary. Then give students a few minutes to read the box. Practice the rising and falling intonation with the whole class using the example sentences.

1 After students have listened to the audio, check their answers by drilling the whole class on the intonation patterns.

AUDIO SCRIPT 1.26

1 What are those?
2 Are these your shoes?
3 Is this price correct?
4 When do you close?

ANSWERS

1 ⌒↘
2 ↗
3 ↗
4 ⌒↘

2 Monitor students as they write their questions, and check the grammatical structure and sense of their questions. After they have practiced the questions and answers with a partner, ask two pairs to model their short conversations.

Speaking skill

Before asking students to read the *Talking about prices* box, write the two questions on the board with the words in a random order. For example, write: *this / is / how / much / ? much / these / are / how / ?*

Ask students to put them in the correct order and then read the box. After that, elicit any other currencies they know and write them on the board. Using these currencies or the ones in the box, write a selection of prices on the board. For example, write: *55.76 dollars/ cents, 76.50 euros/cents, 29.99 pounds/pence.*

Ask students to tell you both the long and short form of each price. You can also point out that English always uses a decimal point in such figures to separate the dollars and cents. The decimal point is never read out.

1 Check that the students know the name of each item. Then play the audio and ask students to write the prices.

AUDIO SCRIPT 1.27

1
A: How much is this?
B: It's sixty-nine dollars and fifty cents.
2
C: How much are these?
D: They're one hundred and twelve dollars.
3
A: How much is this?
B: It's on sale. It's ninety-seven dollars and twenty-five cents.
4
C: How much is this?
D: One-fifty.
5
A: How much are these?
B: They're eighty-nine ninety-nine.

ANSWERS

1 $69.50
2 $112
3 $97.25
4 $1.50
5 $89.99

2 After students have done this task, ask one or two pairs to tell you the price of their things. Write the prices on the board and do further practice with saying these prices.

SPEAKING TASK

This task reviews many of the points covered previously. Before students read the two conversations, check their understanding of *this, that, these,* and *those* by choosing some items around the class to exemplify the concept. Point at the items and use the appropriate pronoun, then ask students to point at other things around the room and decide whether they need to use *this, that, these,* or *those.*

Write two questions on the board. One should be a *wh-* question and the other a *yes/no* question. Elicit which is the *wh-* question and which is the *yes/no* question. Then ask students to work individually to complete the task.

ANSWERS

Conversation 1

Salesclerk: <u>Can I help you?</u>
Customer: Yes. <u>How much is [this] shirt?</u>
Salesclerk: It's twenty dollars.
Customer: <u>What size is it?</u>
Salesclerk: It's a medium.
Customer: Oh.
Salesclerk: <u>Do you want to try it on?</u>
Customer: No, that's OK. <u>Where is the sporting goods section?</u>
Salesclerk: It's on the fourth floor.

Conversation 2

Salesclerk: <u>Can I help you?</u>
Customer: Yes. <u>How much are [these] sunglasses?</u>
Salesclerk: They're $12.
Customer: <u>Do you have them in blue?</u>
Salesclerk: No, I'm sorry. But [those] sunglasses over there come in blue.
Customer: Oh, [those] are nice. <u>How much are they?</u>
Salesclerk: They're $169.
Customer: Um, I'll keep looking.

Brainstorm and plan

Review the names of the items in the pictures. Have students work in partners, with one being the salesclerk and the other the customer. Tell the salesclerks to think of a price for each item and the customer to think of two follow up questions about each product. You might want to model one as an example by giving questions to students such as: *Do you have this in black? Do you have it in a bigger size?*

Ask students to work in pairs to do the task in the *Plan* section. This could be extended to be multiple conversations depending on the range of questions students thought of in the *Brainstorm* section.

Speak and share

While students are practicing the conversations, monitor their use of *this, that, these,* and *those* as well as their use of intonation. Drill any problem intonation patterns you notice.

Ask pairs to perform their conversations for the class. As with the *Speak* section, you could drill and practice the intonation patterns as an extension to this exercise. During this stage, monitor and take language notes. Use the photocopiable *Unit assignment checklist* on page 91 to assess the students' speaking.

STUDY SKILLS What are my personal resources?

This page is from Palgrave's *The Study Skills Handbook* by Stella Cottrell. As well as *The Study Skills Handbook,* there are many other useful titles in the series, covering topics such as exam preparation and critical thinking.

Cultural awareness

In some countries, the idea of a counseling service might seem quite alien. Students might not be comfortable discussing such issues as each society has different ways of dealing with personal issues.

This particular task requires students to organize ideas as a mind map. This type of organization of words can be applied to any thought or language process. Students are asked to consider resources that are around them and which could help them in their research skills.

With the class, brainstorm one of the branches of the mind map collectively. Make sure students are clear about the meaning of the words in the mind map. They might not be familiar with the expression *counseling service,* for example. In addition, students may not have conceived of making friends as a resource that is important to further their study skills. When the class has finished checking the meaning of the words, students can complete the mind map individually or with partners. There are no right or wrong answers in this task, but students who struggle to complete the map might have a limited perception of what resources might be available.

EXTENSION ACTIVITY

As an alternative to brainstorming around a mind map, you can put students into groups. Give each group of students enough paper so that they have one sheet each. On each sheet, students write one of the areas, for example, *college.* Each student then adds one item to the list and passes it to their left. Students keep doing this until the group runs out of ideas.

This can be a good method if you have some students who are likely to dominate their groups.

Listening	Listening for times
Vocabulary	Changing nouns to adjectives
Grammar	Simple present tense
Pronunciation	Sentence stress
Speaking	Asking for clarification

Discussion point

Refer students to the picture on page 47, and ask them to divide the foods into fruit and vegetables. Can they read the prices on the labels in the pictures? For example, *4 for 1.00* could be read as *Four for a pound.* (The fact that several of the labels identify the food as English suggests that these shelves are from a British supermarket.) Ask students to discuss the questions with a partner, using the sentence frames to help them get started. Photocopy and cut out the *Useful language* on page 81 to provide some extra support. The answer to the first question in order from top left to bottom right is: apples, lemons, apples, oranges, parsnips, sprouts, carrots, (runner) beans, onions, and potatoes. Follow with a whole-class discussion so students can share their answers.

EXTENSION ACTIVITY

Continue the discussion by asking students to name other countries and the foods they are famous for. You could then expand this into work on checking some common nationalities and countries, e.g., Japan/Japanese, Italy/Italian, etc. Check that the students can name a variety of countries. Also, check that they use the correct stress patterns. The discussion could lead into talk about the popularity of other countries' foods in the students' own countries.

Vocabulary preview 1

Students should be familiar with carrots and potatoes from the previous page, so these could be used as examples. When students have completed this task, ask them to discuss with a partner which foods they like and which ones they eat regularly.

ANSWERS

1 e	4 f	7 k	10 b
2 h	5 l	8 i	11 d
3 j	6 a	9 g	12 c

LISTENING 1 Mealtime habits

Before you listen

When students have discussed the questions in pairs, ask one pair to share their responses; write the names of the food on the board. Ask other students if they have anything different and write these on the board. Try to build up a large selection of vocabulary for students to use.

EXTENSION ACTIVITY

Have students classify the foods from the discussion, e.g., meats, drinks, vegetables, fruits, cereals, etc.

For question 2, you might need to pre-teach a few concepts for students to be able to explain the reasons why they do not eat certain foods. For example, health and allergies, religion, disliking something, ethical reasons, etc.

Global listening

Before you play the audio, check the students can pronounce the names of the different countries correctly. Ask students to discuss with a partner what they know about each country. They should try to think of two things for each country. It doesn't matter if it is food related, but if they know something, then they should share it with the class.

AUDIO SCRIPT   1.28
Spain

Reporter: What do you eat for breakfast in Spain, Cristina?

Cristina: Breakfast is small. We have coffee with milk, bread, and sometimes cheese. Lunch is our main meal. We have bread, meat or fish, and potatoes and other vegetables. We have it between one thirty and three thirty or so. Oh, we also have something called *la merienda.*

Reporter: What does that mean exactly?

Cristina: It's a snack, I guess. It's between half past four and five o'clock or so. That's because we eat dinner late—between nine and midnight.

Reporter: Wow! And what do you have for dinner?

Cristina: Fish, seafood, or meat. And potatoes, rice, vegetables, fruit—lots of things!

Japan

Reporter: What's breakfast like in Japan, Masao?

Masao: We have rice, fish, soup, and green tea.

Reporter: Fish for breakfast? Wow! What about lunch?

Masao: We have that between noon and about one o'clock. We have noodles a lot. And rice dishes.

Reporter: Is dinner your main meal?

Masao: I think so. It's from six to eight or so. For dinner we have fish, seafood, or meat, plus rice and soup. But it depends. Not everyone eats that. Western food is popular, too.

Russia

Reporter: What are meals like in Russia, Anna?

Anna: Breakfast is small and fast. We just have tea or coffee, juice, bread. And … a kind of thick cereal.

Reporter: A thick cereal? Can you explain that?

Anna: It's a hot cereal. You add hot water and mix it.

Reporter: Oh, I see. And what do you have for lunch and dinner?

Anna: Lunch is from one to two o'clock or so. It's our main meal. We have salad, soup, meat or fish, potatoes, other vegetables, and bread. Dinner is from seven to eight thirty. We have salad, bread, fish, meat, tea—oh, and we eat caviar. You know, fish eggs. Delicious!

Oman

Reporter: Tell us about breakfast in Oman, Ahmed.

Ahmed: Breakfast is a small meal. We have bread and tea or coffee.

Reporter: And for lunch?

Ahmed: Lunch is our main meal. It's from around noon to three, and we have rice with meat or fish. Plus we have thin breads, salads, soup, and coffee or yogurt drinks. Dinner is late—from seven o'clock to approximately ten. It's a light meal. We have similar things to lunch. Fruit is also popular at night, and tea or coffee, of course.

ANSWERS

	Breakfast	Lunch	Dinner
Spain		✓	
Japan			✓
Russia		✓	
Oman		✓	

EXTENSION ACTIVITY

Breakfasts are obviously very varied around the world. Show students a range of pictures of breakfasts from different countries. Ask them to guess the countries and to name any of the foods they can see. For variety, the following could be good examples:

Dim Sum: a range of small plates often containing vegetables, rice, and fish (China)

Changua: a soup made from eggs, scallions, and milk (Colombia)

Croissants and coffee (France)

Idli: a cake made from lentils, served with chutney and vegetable stew (India)

Miso soup: usually served with rice and pickles (Japan)

Sirniki: cheese pancakes (Russia)

Arous labnah: rolled flat bread with soft cheese (Lebanon)

Some of these foods are eaten in more than just the countries listed, for example, croissants and arous labnah are found in many countries.

Ask students which ones are most like their own breakfast and which they would prefer to eat.

Close listening

1 Before you play the audio again, ask students to try to correct any mistakes they can from memory.

ANSWERS
1 People drink coffee with milk for breakfast.
2 *La merienda* is eaten before dinner. / *La merienda* is eaten after lunch.
3 Breakfast is rice, fish, soup, and green tea.
4 For lunch, noodles and rice dishes are popular.
5 Breakfast is small and fast.
6 Fish eggs are popular.
7 People have bread with tea or coffee for breakfast.
8 Fruit is popular at night.

Before referring students to the *Listening for times* box, write a number of different times on the board and elicit how to say each time. For example, write: *9:45, 10:10, 11:15, 12:30, 3:20.* Make sure students practice all ways of saying the time.

Cultural awareness

The use of a 24-hour clock varies between countries. In some countries, it is more common in writing to use the 24-hour clock. For example, *20:00* rather than *8:00 p.m.* In others, it is only in certain situations where it is used, such as with train and bus timetables or medical appointments. In the U.S., the 24-hour clock is rarely used. Ask students when they typically use the 24-hour clock in their own country.

2 Elicit what times the students remember before playing the extracts. Then check the answers with the class.

AUDIO SCRIPT 1.29
1 We eat dinner late—between nine and midnight.
2 **Reporter:** What about lunch?
  Masao: We have that between noon and about one o'clock.
3 Dinner is from seven to eight thirty. We have salad, bread, fish, meat, tea.
4 Lunch is our main meal. It's from around noon to three, and we have rice with meat or fish.

Taste

ANSWERS
1 between 9:00 and midnight/12 a.m.
2 between noon/12 p.m. and 1:00
3 between 7:00 and 8:30
4 between noon/12 p.m. and 3:00

Over to you

In a monolingual class, discuss question 1 with the whole class and see if everyone can agree on the typical time. In a multilingual class, compare the variety of times from different nationalities.

After students have discussed question 2 in pairs, as a class try to find out which meal is the favorite one for the majority of students and why. Write the answers on the board.

Vocabulary preview 2

1 Check that students know the different types of foods in each picture and then have them label them using the words in the box. Depending on which country your students are from, some of the answers may vary. Give students the chance to explain why they've chosen to categorize a food with a certain taste.

POSSIBLE ANSWERS

1 sour	6 juicy
2 salty	7 creamy
3 spicy	8 chewy
4 bland	9 crispy
5 sweet	10 oily

2 When students have named one more food for each taste and texture, have them describe food from earlier in the unit with adjectives from exercise 1.

EXTENSION ACTIVITY

Write these sentences on the board and ask students to complete them with words from exercise 1.

1 This food tastes of nothing. It's so _____.
2 These oranges are too _____. I prefer sweet ones.
3 This curry is really _____. It's too hot for me to eat.
4 I don't like _____ sauces. They are too heavy.
5 Is this fish fried? It's really _____.
6 This meat is too _____. It will take me all day to eat it!

LISTENING 2 Street food

Before you listen

Check students are familiar with the term *street food*. Ask them to discuss the questions with a partner. You can add additional questions, such as: *What street foods are popular in your country? Where can you get the best street food in your hometown?*

Global listening

Before playing the audio, have students describe some of the pictures to a partner. Encourage them to use some of the food words they have learned in the class as well as some of the adjectives from the *Vocabulary preview 2* section.

ANSWERS
1 d   2 e   3 c   4 a   5 f   6 b

AUDIO SCRIPT   1.30

1 Claudia

My favorite street snack here in Brazil is cheese bread. They are little balls of bread, and we eat them as a snack, but also for breakfast. They're very soft and chewy, and also a little bit sour. They taste like cheese, of course! We buy them on the street, but these days we also make them at home. They're easy to make.

2 Dennis

In the Philippines, there are some places to get desserts, like halo-halo. *Halo* means "mix." This dish is a mix of ice and sweet milk. To that they add sweet beans, sugar, fruit, and even young rice. It's cold, very sweet, and, with the milk, creamy. You get a big portion, so we often share one.

3 Susanne

In Germany, the pretzel is a popular street food. There are different kinds, but it's all bread. They are in different shapes and sizes, but all of them are chewy. And they put salt on top of them, so they taste pretty salty sometimes. They're great warm and on a cold winter day.

4 Tom

We have a lot of street food in Jamaica. I miss it all, but I really miss jerk chicken. It's very popular, and you see it in Jamaican or Caribbean restaurants, too. We add a lot of spices to the chicken, then we cook it. It's very spicy; very hot. And juicy, too. You can also make jerk fish and other jerk dishes, but jerk chicken is my favorite.

5 Wendy

The french fries you get in Canada are different from other places. They are regular french fries, crispy, oily, salty, but then we add to them. We add cheese and sometimes a brown sauce. Amazing! I don't think they're very healthy, but they're delicious.

6 Les

The Gatsby is a popular street sandwich here in South Africa. No two are the same, but it's basically crispy French bread with meat or fish, plus cheese and salad. What makes a Gatsby different from other sandwiches are the french fries inside it. We put hot sauce on it to make it spicy. Without that it could be bland.

Close listening

1 When you have played the audio again and students have completed the task, have them spell the country to you for you to write on the board. You could also ask students to name and spell the nationalities (Brazilian, Filipino, German, Jamaican, Canadian, and South African). Check and drill the pronunciation if necessary.

ANSWERS

1 Brazil	4 Jamaica
2 the Philippines	5 Canada
3 Germany	6 South Africa

2 Before playing the audio again, elicit the adjectives used to describe each dish. Play the audio to check the students' answers.

ANSWERS

1 soft, chewy, sour	4 spicy, juicy
2 sweet, creamy	5 crispy, oily, salty
3 chewy, salty	6 crispy, spicy

Over to you

Encourage students to choose a favorite among the six street snacks in the *Close listening* section. They could also choose which one(s) they think would sell best in their country.

Vocabulary skill

Write the following sentences on the board: *It is a windy day. There is a lot of wind today.*

Ask students to identify the nouns and adjectives in each sentence. When they have done this, ask students to read the *Changing nouns to adjectives by adding -y* box.

1 After students have written the adjective form of the nouns, have them make sentences using three of the adjectives.

ANSWERS

1 sugary	4 bony
2 cheesy	5 crusty
3 buttery	6 fatty

2 Ask students to work individually to do the task and then check the answers together as a class. Ask students to give you sentences with each adjective and write them on the board.

ANSWERS

1 oil	4 juice
2 taste	5 spice
3 cream	6 salt

3 Tell students that they don't have to choose just one adjective for each picture, as more than one could be possible. Below are some possible answers, but allow any that are logical.

POSSIBLE ANSWERS

1 bony	4 fatty
2 crusty	5 cheesy
3 sugary	6 buttery

4 Have students work in pairs and then report back to the class. Encourage students to give reasons to support their opinions.

EXTENSION ACTIVITY

Put the food vocabulary from the unit onto cards and play a game. Students pick a card and then describe the food on the card. If they describe it without saying the word (i.e. use adjectives), they keep the card. The object is to collect as many cards as possible.

SPEAKING Describing a favorite meal or snack

This is a good place to use the video resource *Eat out or eat in?* It is located in the Video resources section of the digital component. Alternatively, remind the students about the video resource so they can do this at home.

Grammar

Before having students read the *Grammar* box, review when to use the simple present tense. Write one or two examples on the board if necessary.

1 Write the first sentence on the board and together as a class put the words into the correct order. Then ask students to order the other questions. When they have asked the questions to a partner, ask one or two pairs to tell you about their partner. Review the subject-verb relationship if necessary.

ANSWERS
1 Where do you eat in your home?
2 Do people in your country eat a big lunch?
3 Why do people like to eat street food?
4 What time does dinner start?
5 Does fruit have a lot of sugar?
6 Does your teacher allow snacks in class?

2 After students have written the questions, have them ask and answer the questions in pairs.

POSSIBLE ANSWERS
1 Where do you eat lunch?
2 What time do you have lunch?
3 Why does he like nuts?
4 Where does Pam have lunch (every day)?
5 How often do they eat oatmeal for breakfast?
6 What does Ben never drink at night?

3 At the end of the group discussion, ask each group to report back on their responses.

Speaking skill

Before asking students to read the *Asking for clarification* box, you could write the sentences on the board with some words missing. For example, write:

What _____ "spicy" mean?

What _____ do you mean?

Can you _____ that?

Sorry, I don't _____.

Ask students to try and fill in the blanks. Explain when people say these sentences. Then refer students to the box.

1 Give students a few minutes to read the conversations before playing the audio.

> **AUDIO SCRIPT 1.31**
> **1**
> **A:** Dave is a couch potato.
> **B:** What does "couch potato" mean?
> **A:** He just watches TV all day.
> **2**
> **C:** This exam is a piece of cake.
> **D:** What exactly do you mean?
> **C:** Oh, it's very easy.
> **3**
> **A:** Allison has a finger in every pie.
> **B:** I don't follow.
> **A:** She's involved with a lot of different things.
> **4**
> **C:** This book isn't my cup of tea.
> **D:** Can you explain that?
> **C:** I don't like it very much.

> **ANSWERS**
> 1 What does "couch potato" mean?
> 2 What exactly do you mean?
> 3 I don't follow.
> 4 Can you explain that?

2 Have some volunteers practice the conversations in front of the class. You may need to drill the rising intonation on words and sentences to show politeness.

Pronunciation skill

Write the following sentences on the board: *I don't like to eat spicy food. I like to eat creamy desserts in a restaurant.*

In the first sentence, underline the content words and circle the function words. Elicit the same for the second sentence. Then ask students to read the *Sentence stress* box.

1 Have students do this exercise individually, then check the answers in pairs.

> **ANSWERS**
> 1 **A:** He is a <u>bad egg</u>.
>   **B:** I <u>don't follow</u>.
>   **A:** He is a <u>bad person</u>.
> 2 **A:** An <u>apple</u> a <u>day keeps</u> the <u>doctor away</u>.
>   **B:** <u>What</u> do you <u>mean</u>?
>   **A:** <u>Fruit</u> is <u>good</u> for you. It <u>keeps</u> you <u>healthy</u>.

2 Play the audio and ask students to check their answers. Then check collectively as a whole class.

> **AUDIO SCRIPT 1.32**
> **1**
> **A:** He is a bad egg.
> **B:** I don't follow.
> **A:** He is a bad person.
> **2**
> **A:** An apple a day keeps the doctor away.
> **B:** What do you mean?
> **A:** Fruit is good for you. It keeps you healthy.

3 When students have practiced the conversations, ask one or two pairs to model them for the class.

SPEAKING TASK

Do the first sentence of the conversation on the board as an example, and then do two more as a whole class before assigning the task as pair work. Alternatively, you could write or project the conversation on the board with some of the verbs and question words missing for students to complete. For example, write:

Lara: My favorite snack _____ nachos. Nachos _____ crunchy tortilla chips, cheese, beans, meat, and salsa.

Rani: Salsa? _____ you explain that?

Lara: Salsa _____ a spicy mix of tomatoes, onions, and chilies.

Rani: That _____ good.

Lara: I _____ order nachos in restaurants. I like to make my own at home. I make them when we _____ movies with friends. We usually _____ soda with them. I _____ nachos because they are cheesy and delicious, and they're easy to share with friends.

Rani: _____ they healthy?

Lara: Um, I don't _____ so.

ANSWERS

Lara: My favorite snack is nachos. Nachos are crunchy tortilla chips, cheese, beans, meat, and salsa.

Rani: Salsa? Can you explain that?

Lara: Salsa is a spicy mix of tomatoes, onions, and chilies.

Rani: That sounds good.

Lara: I don't order nachos in restaurants. I like to make my own at home. I make them when we watch movies with friends. We usually drink soda with them. I like nachos because they are cheesy and delicious, and they're easy to share with friends.

Rani: Are they healthy?

Lara: Um, I don't think so.

Brainstorm and plan

To exemplify the *Brainstorm* task, you could complete the chart about a snack or meal that you enjoy and share it with the class.

Ask students to prepare what they are going to say in more detail. Monitor and support students in writing their plan.

Speak and share

Choose a pair of students and have them describe their meal to the class. Ask for a lot of clarification (an exaggerated amount) as if you really do not understand what they are saying. Then ask students to practice again, focusing on their sentence stress and using the clarification phrases.

Mix groups up so that different people are working together and then ask students to repeat their descriptions. During this stage, monitor and take language notes. Use the photocopiable *Unit assignment checklist* on page 92 to assess the students' speaking.

STUDY SKILLS Using a learner's dictionary

Background information

Good monolingual dictionaries, such as the Macmillan Study Dictionary, use a corpus as their source, which is a database containing millions of examples of real English as it is used around the world.

Online dictionaries, such as the Macmillan online dictionary, are particularly useful as they are often free to use, include a thesaurus and examples for each entry, and give the pronunciation of each word in both British and American English. Online dictionaries are becoming increasingly popular, and many publishers are now abandoning their print dictionaries in favor of online dictionaries. It is therefore important to

encourage students to get used to using online monolingual dictionaries rather than relying too heavily on bilingual translation dictionaries.

Before starting this activity, ask students to tell a partner how they find out the meaning of unknown words. Then, collect recommendations from the whole class and write them on the board. Encourage students to try a new method from the list in the future.

Getting started

Generate a discussion about different types of dictionary, specifically paper versus digital. You could ask students to complete this sentence: *I prefer to use ... because ...* Students could complete the sentence with a number of reasons.

Ask students to discuss the questions in pairs and then report back their ideas to the class.

Scenario

Give students time to read the scenario and make suggestions for George. Help students with any problem words. You might need to explain the prefix *bi-* and the word *illustration*. Have a whole-class discussion to share ideas.

POSSIBLE ANSWER

Some people argue that bilingual dictionaries are not ideal learning tools for learners, as it doesn't take much effort to understand something that is simply translated. Arguably, though, at a low level they can be helpful. George uses the bilingual dictionary to support him rather than as his main dictionary, which is advisable. However, he should also use a learner's dictionary at home.

Consider it

Have students try to rank the features from the most useful to the least useful. You might need to give them a sentence frame: *X is more/most useful because ...*

Over to you

Ask students to discuss their answers to the questions with a partner, and then open it up to a class discussion.

EXTENSION ACTIVITY

Ask students to try to use a different type of dictionary for the next week. In a future class, ask students to assess how positive or negative they feel about the new dictionary and whether they will continue using it or not.

Play

Listening	Making inferences
Vocabulary	Collocating with *go, play,* and *do*
Grammar	Prepositions of time: *in, at, on*
Pronunciation	Intonation patterns in reactions
Speaking	Reacting appropriately

Discussion point

Refer students to the picture on page 57 and elicit what they can see. It's a roller coaster in the U.S. Ask if they ever go to fairgrounds and where their nearest one is. Write *free-time activities* on the board and ask students to think of some examples.

Ask students to discuss the questions with a partner, using the sentence frames to help them get started. Photocopy and cut out the *Useful language* on page 82 to provide some extra support. After they have discussed the questions, ask one or two students to share their answers with the class.

EXTENSION ACTIVITY

Conduct a "Find someone who …" activity related to free time. Students have to find someone in the class who: has a lot of free time, likes playing sports, likes going shopping, etc. Tell students they should find a different person for each category you give them.

Vocabulary preview 1

1   Draw the students' attention to the pictures and ask them to check the ones they like to do. While doing the exercise, students might ask about using the *-ing* form (e.g., *cooking*). Explain that both forms are grammatically correct and that the meaning is the same.

ANSWERS
1 play sport	5 read
2 run	6 walk
3 cook	7 chat online
4 watch TV	8 play video games

2   Ask students to work in pairs to discuss the activities in exercise 1. Encourage them to give reasons for their answers. Ask students if they could only do two of these activities in the future, which ones they would choose and why. You might like to give students this sentence frame to help them: *I would choose … and … because …* Choose two or three pairs to report back to the class afterwards.

LISTENING 1 A typical day

Before you listen

Discuss with the students the chart comparing free time between countries. Students might need some language support for comparative statistics, for example: *Belgians spend more than a quarter of their day relaxing. Belgians have more free time than Mexicans.* Then ask students to discuss the questions in groups.

EXTENSION ACTIVITY

Ask students to draw a clock that is divided into 24 sections to represent the hours of a day. Then have them color in the different sections to represent how long they spend each day on different activities. For example, if they sleep eight hours a day, they should color in eight sections of their chart in one color. To help, you could give students some typical categories, such as eating, studying, working, watching TV, going online, etc. When students have colored in their chart, have them work with a partner. The pairs ask and answer questions to guess what activity each color represents.

Background information

The Organisation for Economic Co-operation and Development (OECD) aims to promote policies that will improve the economic and social well-being of people around the world. In one of their studies, they created something called "the better life index" which rates countries on things such as housing, jobs, the environment, and education. One of the things it rates is the work-life balance. The average person in the OECD works 1,749 hours per year. They spend 62% of the day, or 14.8 hours, eating, sleeping, socializing, with friends and family, doing hobbies, playing games, and watching TV.

Ask students to think about 24 hours in their life and to think about how much time they spend on different activities. How do they compare to the OECD average?

Global listening

After students listen to the audio and complete the exercise, ask them to discuss with a partner whose typical day sounds most interesting and which one sounds most like their own typical day.

AUDIO SCRIPT 2.01
1 Sophie

I have a lot of free time, about seven hours in a typical day. I like to spend my free time with my friends. After our last class, we like to go shopping or just walk around town before dinner. To be honest, I think I spend most of my time watching TV. Probably around 50% of my free time is spent watching TV—about three hours a day. In a typical day I watch one hour in the morning and two hours at night, after dinner. My major is biology, so I like to watch TV shows about animals and nature.

2 Colin

I have quite a bit of free time these days. In a typical day, I guess I'm free about six hours. I don't really like to watch TV or play video games. I prefer sports. I suppose I spend most of my free time playing sports. I often play soccer or basketball with my friends after class. I also love to play volleyball. We usually play for about three hours. I don't do much in the evening. After I cook dinner, I just read.

3 Kumiko

I'm pretty busy, so I don't have a lot of free time. I think I probably have about five hours in a typical day. After I finish studying, I like to go out with my friends. We love to shop. We don't usually buy very much, though. I spend most of my free time doing that. I also spend time chatting with my friends or talking on the phone. We usually talk about school or what we're planning to do on the weekend.

4 Eduardo

I only have about four hours a day of free time. I live alone, so after I get home from school, I cook dinner and then just relax. I have a blog, so I spend most of my free time writing on that. My friends and family like to read it, so I try to write something every day. I'm a literature major, and I think I want to be a writer someday. I also like to play my guitar in my free time. I'm not very good, but I'm getting better.

ANSWERS
1 c   2 b   3 c   4 b

Close listening

1 Play the audio again and ask students to circle the correct answers. Then check the answers together as a class.

ANSWERS
1 b   2 b   3 b   4 a   5 b   6 b   7 a   8 a

Ask students to read the *Making inferences* box, and then write the following sentences on the board: *I need to go to the bank. Have you seen my keys? Look at the weather forecast! Let's go to the beach on the weekend.*

Elicit what students can infer from each statement. Accept any answers that make sense. Then explain that a sentence needs to be listened to in context to make an inference as it will often relate to other information the speaker has been saying.

2 After you have played the audio and checked the answers, put the sentences from the audio on the board. Ask students which words helped them to make the inference.

AUDIO SCRIPT 2.02
1 I like to spend my free time with my friends. After our last class, we like to go shopping or just walk around town before dinner.
2 I often play soccer or basketball with my friends after class. I also love to play volleyball.
3 I also spend time chatting with my friends or talking on the phone. We usually talk about school or what we're planning to do on the weekend.
4 I live alone, so after I get home from school, I cook dinner and then just relax. I have a blog, so I spend most of my free time writing in that.

ANSWERS
1 Sophie has classes in the afternoon.
2 Colin prefers team sports.
3 Kumiko is a sociable person.
4 Eduardo is single.

Over to you

After the groups of students have discussed the first question, have two students explain their reasons to the class. You could then ask another two students which person they would least like to spend time with and why. For question 2, refer students to the *Activities* box for ideas.

Vocabulary preview 2

1 A number of the nouns in this exercise might be new to students. To help them understand these hobbies, after the students have matched the verbs to the nouns, you could follow up with the *Extension activity* on the next page.

ANSWERS
1 c	4 f	7 h
2 a	5 e	8 i
3 b	6 d	9 g

EXTENSION ACTIVITY

Write some sentences on the board for students to complete using the phrases from exercise 1. For example:

1 I often _____ of my friends and put them on Facebook. (take photos)
2 My grandfather _____ of planes. (builds models)
3 I _____ from different countries around the world. (collect coins)
4 My daughter _____. She loves being with animals. (rides horses)
5 I don't _____. I find the game too slow and boring. (play chess)
6 I like to _____ for my children to read. (write stories)
7 Not many people _____ by hand now, as it is easier to do it with a computer. (do calligraphy)
8 I _____, and give the necklaces and bracelets to friends for their birthdays. (make jewelry)
9 I can't _____. I take mine to a mechanic. (fix cars)

2 After students have discussed the questions with a partner, ask two students to tell the class the hobby they would choose and the reason for the choice. Generate a discussion about the other hobbies.

LISTENING 2 What a hobby!

Before you listen

After the group discussion, find out from the class if anyone has any unusual hobbies that were not mentioned earlier.

This is a good place to use the video resource *Taking hobbies to the extreme*. It is located in the Video resources section of the digital component. Alternatively, remind the students about the video resource so they can do this at home.

Global listening

1 Ask students to look at the pictures and guess what each hobby is. Then play the audio and ask them to number the hobbies in the correct order.

AUDIO SCRIPT 2.03

Host: Hello and welcome to the show. Tonight, I have four guests with me. Each guest has an unusual hobby. First, we have Ted. Ted has an unusual collection. Second, we have Pamela. Pamela makes something unusual. What she makes looks beautiful, and delicious, too. Next, we have Adam. Adam likes to build things. We'll see what that something is. And finally, we have Ling. Someone hides things, and then Ling uses technology to find it.

ANSWERS

1 c 2 d 3 a 4 b

2 Play the audio and check the answers for exercise 1 together as a class.

AUDIO SCRIPT 2.04

Host: So, Ted. What's your hobby?

Ted: I collect dictionaries.

Host: Dictionaries?

Ted: Yeah. I collect bilingual dictionaries—you know, English-Spanish, English-Japanese, English-Arabic. I'm trying to get one dictionary for every country in the world.

Host: How many do you have?

Ted: At last count I have 58.

Host: Wow! That's a lot. But aren't there more than 58 languages in the world?

Ted: Right, many more, but not every language is written, or has an English dictionary. And I'm still collecting.

Host: I see. You have some very interesting ones here. So how many languages do you speak?

Ted: Me? Just one.

Host: Now let's meet Pamela.

Pamela: Hello.

Host: Tell us about your hobby.

Pamela: My hobby is making things from fruit and vegetables. I make them look like flowers, or people— anything really.

Host: What do you do this for?

Pamela: Just for fun. I like being creative. I even make things for friends, as gifts.

Host: Do you do it alone?

Pamela: Yes, but sometimes my mother helps out.

Host: That's nice. Do you ever eat your creations after?

Pamela: Um, no, never.

Host: My third guest is Adam. Adam likes to build things.

Adam: That's right. But only one thing.

Host: And what's that?

Adam: Robots. I build them with my brother.

Host: Robots? Can regular people actually build robots?

Adam: Sure, simple ones. You just need to find the parts. It's easy.

Host: Really? It sounds really hard.

Adam: Well, here's one I made. What do you think?

Host: Well, it looks very interesting …

Adam: It has a battery, and I make it move with a remote control. Here, I'll make it move. Um, wait, something isn't working …

Host: My last guest is Ling. Ling's hobby is … well, you explain it.

Ling: I do geocaching.

Host: Geocaching. What is geocaching exactly?

Ling: It's a kind of game, a hide and seek game. People use a GPS to search for and find an object.

Host: Sorry, I don't understand.

Ling: OK. First, you sign up online and choose a geocache to find. You put information into a GPS and then look for the object. They are often in unusual places, so you really need to look.

Host: What does a geocache look like?

Ling: It's usually in a bag or a box. There's a little log book with it. After you find it, you sign the log book and put it back for someone else to find. It sounds strange, but it's actually a lot of fun.

Close listening

Before playing the audio again, have the students try to recall or guess the missing information.

> **ANSWERS**
>
> | | |
> |---|---|
> | 1 bilingual | 5 brother |
> | 2 58 | 6 parts |
> | 3 gifts | 7 GPS |
> | 4 mother | 8 sign |

Over to you

Before asking the students to discuss the questions in groups, have them put actual ages next to each age group. Elicit these ages and write them on the board. Try to get the students to agree on a rough age range to describe each group.

Vocabulary skill

Write these three sentences on the board and ask students to correct the mistakes: *I like to play running. I like to do chess. I like to go karate.* (Answers: *I like to go running. I like to play chess. I like to do karate.*)

Refer students to the *Collocating with go, play, and do* box.

1 Check students know the meaning of all the activities in the box and then ask them to complete the chart.

> **ANSWERS**
>
> | go + _____ | play + _____ | do + _____ |
> |---|---|---|
> | bowling | badminton | aerobics |
> | jogging | the guitar | taekwondo |
> | skating | tennis | yoga |
> | swimming | | |

2 After students have compared their charts, ask one pair to give you their answers. Elicit from the class any other activities that they added to the chart. Write these on the board.

3 Monitor and check students are using the correct forms as they are discussing the activities in exercise 1; highlight any errors on the board.

EXTENSION ACTIVITY

You may want to do this later in the class or on a different day as a revision activity.

Write incorrect collocations onto the board and ask students to correct them. For example, write:

play yoga

do tennis

do jogging

go aerobics

SPEAKING Interviewing a classmate about free time

Grammar

Before asking students to read the *Grammar* box, write these sentences on the board:

My birthday is _____ January. Lunch is _____ one o'clock. I don't teach _____ Thursday.

Try to elicit any rules students know about the three prepositions and then ask them to read the box.

1 After students have written the words in the correct columns, ask them to add one more example to each column.

> **ANSWERS**
>
> | in | at | on |
> |---|---|---|
> | 1999 | 10:15 | 06/24/2013 |
> | the afternoon | night | December 12th |
> | September | noon | Friday |
> | the spring | | the morning of May 1st |
> | | | New Year's Day |

2 When students have finished completing the sentences, ask two students to tell the class about their partner.

EXTENSION ACTIVITY

Tell students to have a piece of paper and a pen ready. Tell them you are going to say a list of times and that they must write down the correct preposition. Read the following list out very quickly to students.

1 October (in)

2 2012 (in)

3 12:30 (at)

4 Thursday (on)

5 May 29th (on)

6 the morning (in)

7 Friday morning (on)

8 night (at)

Speaking skill

> ### Background information
> It's important that students learn speaking strategies early, as it is something that can help non-native speakers sound more natural. Encourage students to use synonyms as well, as these are quite a natural feature of English. For example: *It's nice weather today, isn't it?* → *Yes, it's wonderful.*

Before asking students to read the *Reacting appropriately* box, ask one student to tell you about one of their hobbies and react in an interested/surprised way. Then repeat the activity with two more students, and react positively and negatively to each. Elicit what students noticed about your reaction, and then model the intonation pattern.

1 Ask students to read the statements and circle the best response. Then play the audio.

> **AUDIO SCRIPT   2.05**
> 1
> **A:** I do calligraphy five times a week.
> **B:** Really?
> 2
> **A:** I don't do taekwondo anymore. The classes are too expensive.
> **B:** That's terrible.
> 3
> **A:** I make and sell jewelry. I make a lot of money.
> **B:** That's nice.
> 4
> **A:** Let's go skiing. I have free ski rental.
> **B:** How wonderful!
> 5
> **A:** I like to go swimming in the summer.
> **B:** Oh, yeah?

> **ANSWERS**
> 1 a   2 b   3 a   4 a   5 a

2 After pairs of students have practiced the exchanges in exercise 1 together, ask one pair to model each exchange for the whole class.

Pronunciation skill

Ask students to read the *Intonation patterns in reactions* box, and then drill the reactions with the class.

1 Before playing the audio, say three more responses with varying intonation patterns and ask students which pattern you used. Then play the audio and ask students to check the correct intonation pattern.

> **AUDIO SCRIPT   2.06**
> 1
> **A:** My parents can't come to my wedding.
> **B:** How terrible!
> 2
> **A:** I got 100% on my test.
> **B:** Really?
> 3
> **A:** I don't have to work tomorrow.
> **B:** That's nice.
> 4
> **A:** I'm going to be a little late tomorrow.
> **B:** That's fine.
> 5
> **A:** I think I lost my house key.
> **B:** Seriously?
> 6
> **A:** Look! I got engaged!
> **B:** How fantastic!

> **ANSWERS**
>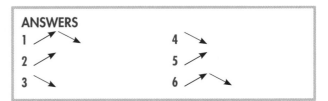

2 Monitor as students do the task in pairs. Choose some students with good use of intonation to present to the class their short conversations.

SPEAKING TASK

After students have read the interview and done the task, ask them to close their books. Write the sentences with prepositions from the interview on the board and leave a blank where the preposition should be. Have students complete the blanks.

> **ANSWERS**
> **Interviewer:** Do you have a lot of free time?
> **Keltoum:** No, not really. I only have about three free hours a day.
> **Interviewer:** <u>That's too bad.</u> On a typical day, what do you do in your free time?
> **Keltoum:** Well, I like to play computer games. I play with my friends.
> **Interviewer:** <u>Oh yeah?</u> When do you play? Do you play in the afternoon?
> **Keltoum:** No, we play at night. We play on weekdays.
> **Interviewer:** <u>That's interesting.</u> Where do you play?
> **Keltoum:** I usually play in my bedroom.
> **Interviewer:** So what else do you do in your free time?
> **Keltoum:** I collect seashells. I have about 500 of them.
> **Interviewer:** <u>Wow!</u> That's amazing! Why do you collect seashells?
> **Keltoum:** I don't know. They're just beautiful, I guess.

Brainstorm

1 If you did the *Extension activity* in the *Listening 1* section about 24 hours in your day, you could refer to this and ask students which activities are related to free time. If not, do this task as explained in the Student's Book.

2 In both cases, ask students to add notes about the activities using the prompts. Give an example, such as: *Who do you play soccer with?*

Plan

Check students' question forms as they ask their partner about their free-time activities. Write the correct forms on the board as needed.

Speak and share

Model an interview with a student first, focusing on your use of intonation in the response. It may help to slightly exaggerate it first. Ask students to do the task. Monitor and then choose one pair to perform their conversation for the class.

Put students into groups for the *Share* activity. Encourage them to react as much as possible while they listen to others. During this stage, monitor and take language notes. Use the photocopiable *Unit assignment checklist* on page 93 to assess the students' speaking.

STUDY SKILLS Doing a web search

Background information

Encouraging students to read in English is a great way to improve their vocabulary. If students read for just one hour a day, they will typically be exposed to four to five million words per day. Reading in volume is a great way for students to improve many language skills, so the more you can encourage them the better. Some studies also show that it is better when students have control over what they choose to read as they are more enthusiastic about the subject. Searching for information on the web is an excellent way for students to increase the amount that they read, and for them to retain control of exactly what they read and when.

Write four or five things on the board and ask students what they would choose if they could only have two of the things. For example, write: *TV, cars, the Internet, phones*. Ask them how they would feel if they had no access to the Internet for a week.

Getting started

Have students discuss the questions either in pairs or as a quick class discussion.

Scenario

Give students time to read the scenario and make suggestions for Tanya. Help students with any problem words. Have a whole-class discussion to share ideas.

POSSIBLE ANSWER

Tanya only needs to type "English learner dictionary" (and inside quotation marks) in her first web search. The fewer the words used, the more accurate the search. In her second web search, she is right to put the book title in quotation marks, but she should also include the year of publication for a more precise search. In her third web search, it is good that she uses the minus sign to exclude what she does not want to search. However, it is not good practice to use the first information she finds on the web. She should ask herself questions such as *Who wrote this? Are they an expert? When was this written? Is it academic?* She should then double-check the information on at least one more website.

Consider it

After students have discussed the tips with a partner, open the discussion to the whole class. Ask students which tips they use already.

Over to you

Have students discuss the questions with a partner. Write all of the students' tips for question 2 on the board and try to create a class "Internet research skills guide." If students have lots of good ideas, you could type it up and circulate it.

Extra research task

Ask students to find out more information from the Internet about free time in their countries. Remind them to practice the web search skills they have learned in the lesson.

UNIT 7 PLACES

Listening	Listening for and following directions
Vocabulary	Writing definitions
Grammar	*Can*
Pronunciation	Linking sounds
Speaking	Using signal words to order information

Discussion point

Ask students to look at the picture on page 67 and talk about it with a partner. You could give them these questions as a guide: *What might be good about living in this city? Does the city look similar to one in your country? Do you prefer living in a small town or a big city?*

Then ask students to discuss the questions with a partner, using the sentence frames to help them get started. Photocopy and cut out the *Useful language* on page 83 to provide some extra support. After they have discussed the questions, ask one or two students to share their answers with the class. You could then extend the activity by asking students to discuss cities they have visited and name which one is their favorite.

This is a good place to use the video resource *In the city*. It is located in the Video resources section of the digital component. Alternatively, remind the students about the video resource so they can do this at home.

Vocabulary preview 1

1   Before asking students to do the task, briefly brainstorm on the board with students different shops and facilities you can find in a local neighborhood. When the students have finished, check the answers with the class.

> **ANSWERS**
> 1 b   2 a   3 b   4 a   5 b
> 6 a   7 a   8 b   9 a

2   Ask students to work with a partner to do the task. Have students report their ideas back to you and write them on the board to help students build up a range of vocabulary.

3   Review vocabulary for describing places, such as *near, far, next to, between, behind, in front of.* Then ask students to work with a partner to discuss their neighborhood.

LISTENING 1   Is it far?

Before you listen

In this task, be prepared for students to simply say *Look on Google maps* or *Use a GPS.* Remind them to use the prompts given when they discuss the question.

Global listening

1   Before playing the audio, elicit where any of the places in the pictures might be. The speakers could be tourists in another country. The post office and the double-decker bus are quite typical designs found in the U.K., so students might recognize them. If they do, ask if anyone has been to the U.K., where they went, and what they did. Then play the audio and ask students to number the pictures.

> **AUDIO SCRIPT   2.07**
> **1**
> **A:** Excuse me.
> **B:** Yes.
> **A:** I'm looking for a bus stop. Is there one near here?
> **2**
> **C:** Sorry to bother you, but is there a bookstore in this neighborhood?
> **D:** A bookstore? Yes. There's one on First Avenue.
> **3**
> **B:** Can I help you?
> **A:** Yes, I'm looking for the train station. Is it near here?
> **4**
> **D:** Excuse me. Is there an ATM near here?
> **C:** An ATM? Yes …
> **5**
> **A:** Can I help you, sir?
> **B:** Yes, thanks. I'm looking for the post office.

> **ANSWERS**
> 1 c   2 a   3 e   4 d   5 b

2   Check students understand the concept of *near* and *far*, and then play the audio.

> **AUDIO SCRIPT   2.08**
> **1**
> **A:** Excuse me.
> **B:** Yes.
> **A:** I'm looking for a bus stop. Is there one near here?
> **B:** Oh yes, it isn't far.
> **A:** Oh, great. I'm really late.
> **B:** OK, um, first, go this way. This is Oak Street. Follow Oak Street until you get to Fourth Avenue.
> **A:** Fourth Avenue?
> **B:** Right. Then turn left. There's a bus stop there, next to a school. It will be on your left.
> **A:** Oh, that's very near. Thanks so much.
> **B:** You're welcome.

2

C: Sorry to bother you, but is there a bookstore in this neighborhood?

D: A bookstore? Yes. There's one on First Avenue.

C: First?

D: Yeah. So go this way, down Oak Street to First Avenue. Then turn right.

C: So I take a right on First?

D: Yes. After that, go up First until you see the bookstore. It's on the right, on the corner of First Avenue and Maple Street. It's next to a stationery store. It isn't far.

C: OK, got it. Thanks a lot.

D: No problem.

3

B: Can I help you?

A: Yes, I'm looking for the train station. Is it near here?

B: Not really. It's pretty far, but you can walk there. First, walk up Second Avenue. Walk for about ten minutes or so. Continue straight until you see a supermarket. Turn right at the supermarket.

A: OK.

B: Then continue until you see the train station. It's on the corner of Elm Street and Fourth Avenue. It's next to a tech store.

A: Thanks for your help.

4

D: Excuse me. Is there an ATM near here?

C: An ATM? Yes, it's very near. Just walk up this street, Second Avenue. It's after Pine Street.

D: OK.

C: It will be on your left. It's next to a drugstore.

D: That sounds easy. Thanks!

5

A: Can I help you, sir?

B: Yes, thanks. I'm looking for the post office.

A: Let's see … OK, well, this is Oak Street.

B: Right …

A: Go this way, to Third Avenue. Then take a left.

B: A left on Third.

A: Uh-huh. And after that, walk up Third Street. Keep going straight until you get to Elm Street. The post office is on the corner of Elm and Third.

B: Hmm, it sounds far. Is it on the right or left?

A: It will be on the left, next to a supermarket.

B: Great. Thank you.

ANSWERS
1 near   2 near   3 far   4 near   5 far

Close listening

Ask the students to read the *Listening for and following directions* box. Check for understanding by giving students directions from your classroom to a location nearby and ask them to tell you where this location is.

For some classes, you may have to play the first conversation and pause it to check students understand the exercise.

ANSWERS
1 bus stop (on Fourth Avenue, next to school)
2 bookstore (on corner of First Avenue and Maple Street, next to stationery store)
3 train station (on corner of Elm Street and Fourth Avenue, next to tech store)
4 ATM (on Second Avenue, next to drugstore)
5 post office (on corner of Elm Street and Third Avenue, next to supermarket)

EXTENSION ACTIVITY

Get students to practice asking for and giving directions using the map in the Student's Book. Change the starting point each time.

Over to you

After students have answered the questions in groups, expand the discussion to include these questions: *Do you get lost often? Are you good at directions? Do you think technology means people don't need to ask for directions?*

Vocabulary preview 2

1 After students have labeled the pictures, generate a discussion about three other tourist activities that they can think of.

ANSWERS
1 market	5 aquarium
2 theater	6 tower
3 zoo	7 amusement park
4 botanical garden	8 stadium

2 Have students discuss the places in exercise 1 in pairs. Encourage them to say more about the places in their city or a city they know well by writing the following prompts on the board: *Where is the …? Do you like the …? How much does it cost to go to the …?*

LISTENING 2 New to Australia

Before you listen

Elicit what students know about Australia. If they seem knowledgeable, have a mini-quiz about Australia using the information in the *Background information* box.

Background information

Facts about Australia

Capital: Canberra

Currency: Australian dollar

Population: 22,991,000 (in 2013, according to the Australian Bureau of Statistics http://www.abs.gov.au)

Official language: English

Vehicles drive on the left

Hosted the Olympics® in Melbourne in 1956 and Sydney in 2000

Natural attractions: the Great Barrier Reef, Ayers Rock, the Tasmanian Wilderness, Kangaroo Island, etc.

Unique animals: kangaroo, emu, koala, platypus, Tasmanian devil, etc.

Global listening

1   Check that students know the pronunciation of the attractions to help them spot them in the audio. Then play the audio and have them number the attractions.

AUDIO SCRIPT   2.09

Roommate: So how do you like Sydney so far, Kenichi?

Kenichi: I don't really know. I've been so busy with classes I haven't seen anything.

Roommate: Really? Nothing at all?

Kenichi: I know there's a lot to do here. Where do I start?

Roommate: Well, if you want to spend a day sightseeing, first, go down to Circular Quay and visit the Opera House.

Kenichi: Can I see the Harbor Bridge from there?

Roommate: Sure. That's a great place to take photos of both. You know, you can climb the bridge with a guide. It's very popular. But it costs about two hundred dollars.

Kenichi: Wow! Two hundred dollars? No, thanks.

Roommate: The Royal Botanical Gardens are nearby, and they're free. You can have a nice walk there and then after that, you can visit the zoo.

Kenichi: Oh, yeah? I love zoos.

Roommate: OK. So walk back to Circular Quay and take the ferry to Taronga Zoo. The boats around the harbor aren't expensive. At the zoo, you can see kangaroos, wombats, koalas, …

Kenichi: That sounds great.

Roommate: Then come back on the ferry and walk around downtown. You could go up Sydney Tower. You can get a great view of the city from there. It costs $26, but it's only $18 if you get a ticket online. Another good place is the State Theater. It's one of Sydney's oldest theaters. You can look around inside for free.

Kenichi: I think that's enough for one day.

ANSWERS

1 Opera House	4 Taronga Zoo
2 Harbor Bridge	5 Sydney Tower
3 Royal Botanical Gardens	6 State Theater

2   Check students know the pronunciation of these places before playing the audio.

AUDIO SCRIPT   2.10

Roommate: Well, there's more to see. On another day, I would start at the Queen Victoria Building. That's a great place to shop and have something to eat.

Kenichi: OK. Um, is there an aquarium in Sydney?

Roommate: Sydney Aquarium is actually really near. It's a great place, but it can get crowded with schoolchildren. It's $36, but online tickets are cheaper—you can buy them for $25. From the aquarium, you can walk or take a taxi to the Fish Market. Oh, be sure to try the fish and chips there. I reckon they are the best in Sydney.

Kenichi: OK, sounds good. Is the Olympic Stadium downtown?

Roommate: No, it's outside the city center.

Kenichi: And what is Luna Park? My guidebook mentions it.

Roommate: Oh, it's a small amusement park. It's on the other side of the harbor. It's OK, but it's kind of old.

Kenichi: And what about Bondi Beach? I know that's quite famous. Is that far from the city center?

Roommate: A little. It's about a 30-minute bus ride. But it's a nice place. It's very popular with tourists. You know, Kenichi, I don't get into the city very much these days. Let's go in this weekend, and I'll show you around.

Kenichi: Really? Thanks!

ANSWERS

7 Queen Victoria Building
8 Sydney Aquarium
9 Fish Market
10 Olympic Stadium
11 Luna Park
12 Bondi Beach

Close listening

Before playing the audio, ask the students to read the questions and to try to recall or guess the answers.

AUDIO SCRIPT   2.11

Roommate: So how do you like Sydney so far, Kenichi?

Kenichi: I don't really know. I've been so busy with classes I haven't seen anything.

Roommate: Really? Nothing at all?

Kenichi: I know there's a lot of to do here. Where do I start?

Roommate: Well, if you want to spend a day sight-seeing, first, go down to Circular Quay and visit the Opera House.

Kenichi: Can I see the Harbor Bridge from there?

Roommate: Sure. That's a great place to take photos of both. You know, you can climb the bridge with a guide. It's very popular. But it costs about two hundred dollars.

Kenichi: Wow! Two hundred dollars? No, thanks.

Roommate: The Royal Botanical Gardens are nearby, and they're free. You can have a nice walk there and then after that, you can visit the zoo.

Kenichi: Oh, yeah? I love zoos.

Roommate: OK. So walk back to Circular Quay and take the ferry to Taronga Zoo. The boats around the harbor aren't expensive. At the zoo, you can see kangaroos, wombats, koalas, …

Kenichi: That sounds great.

Roommate: Then come back on the ferry and walk around downtown. You could go up Sydney Tower. You can get a great view of the city from there. It costs $26, but it's only $18 if you get a ticket online. Another good place is the State Theater. It's one of Sydney's oldest theaters. You can look around inside for free.

Kenichi: I think that's enough for one day.

Roommate: Well, there's more to see. On another day, I would start at the Queen Victoria Building. That's a great place to shop and have something to eat.

Kenichi: OK. Um, is there an aquarium in Sydney?

Roommate: Sydney Aquarium is actually really near. It's a great place, but it can get crowded with schoolchildren. It's $36, but online tickets are cheaper—you can buy them for $25. From the aquarium, you can walk or take a taxi to the Fish Market. Oh, be sure to try the fish and chips there. I reckon they are the best in Sydney.

Kenichi: OK, sounds good. Is the Olympic Stadium downtown?

Roommate: No, it's outside the city center.

Kenichi: And what is Luna Park? My guidebook mentions it.

Roommate: Oh, it's a small amusement park. It's on the other side of the harbor. It's OK, but it's kind of old.

Kenichi: And what about Bondi Beach? I know that's quite famous. Is that far from the city center?

Roommate: A little. It's about a 30-minute bus ride. But it's a nice place. It's very popular with tourists. You know, Kenichi, I don't get into the city very much these days. Let's go in this weekend, and I'll show you around.

Kenichi: Really? Thanks!

ANSWERS

1 a   2 a   3 b   4 b   5 b   6 a   7 b   8 b

Background information

At the time of writing, the Australian dollar was roughly one to one with the U.S. dollar.

Over to you

Have students discuss the questions in groups and then report back to the class. Find out which places students rate the most and least popular in Sydney. For question 2, if students can't think of many interesting places for their own town, then they could choose another location in their country.

Vocabulary skill

Have students close their books. Write on the board the definitions of the three words in the *Writing definitions* box. Review the parts of speech and ask students to guess from the definitions what the parts of speech of the three words are. Then ask students to guess the words.

1   Have students open their books and read the *Writing definitions* box before completing exercise 1. Check the answers together as a class.

ANSWERS

1 adj.; e	4 n.; a
2 v.; f	5 v.; d
3 n.; b	6 adj.; c

2   When students have completed the definitions, ask them to write a definition of something in the room. Each student should then read out their definition, and the rest of the class have to guess what the word is.

ANSWERS

1 buy paper	5 watch sports
2 get money	6 see fish
3 borrow books	7 see a play
4 buy groceries	8 see animals

SPEAKING Describing and giving directions to a place

Grammar

Have students close their books. Write the example sentences in the *Grammar* box on the board. Also, write down the different uses of *can* in a different order. Tell students to match the uses to the sentences. Finally, ask students to read the *Grammar* box and check their guesses.

1   After the students have completed the sentences and checked the answers, ask them to write one example sentence for each of the uses of *can* in the *Grammar* box.

ANSWERS

1 can	5 Can
2 Can	6 can't
3 can't	7 can't
4 can't	8 can't

2 Encourage students to give answers that make sense when they discuss the places in the box. Ask students to report back their answers.

3 Encourage students to give more information about each ability they describe. For example, if a student says they can drive, ask them to tell you something related to it (e.g., if they are fast or careful drivers, and if they have ever had an accident), or if they say they can swim, ask about how often and where they go swimming.

Speaking skill

Write the following paragraph on the board with the underlined words replaced by blanks. Ask students to complete the sentences.

First, walk along Eliot Street. Turn right onto Rotherfield Way. Then/Next, walk for ten minutes until you see a library. After that, you'll find a supermarket on your right.

Have students read the *Using signal words to order information* box.

1 Before playing the audio, ask students to read the conversation and try to predict the word that will fill each blank.

AUDIO SCRIPT 2.12

A: You look lost. Can I help you?

B: Yes, thank you. I'm looking for the State Theater.

A: OK. Well, first, this is Ash Street here. Follow Ash Street for about five minutes and then take a right at Tenth Street.

B: Sorry. Can you repeat that? Tenth Street?

A: That's right. And turn right at Tenth Street.

B: OK.

A: So ... next, look for Elm Street. And after that, turn left. And walk down Elm until you see the State Theater. You can't miss it.

B: Got it. Thank you so much.

ANSWERS

1 first	3 X	5 after that
2 then	4 next	6 X

2 After students have practiced in pairs, invite volunteers to present their conversations to the class.

3 Some students may have difficulty with this task. Check the order together before asking students to tell a partner the directions.

Ask students to write some brief directions from one place to another using the map on page 69. Make sure they use signal words also.

ANSWERS

1 We're at the corner of Oak Street and Second Avenue.
2 Walk up Second Avenue.
3 Go straight until you get to Elm Street.
4 Take a right at Elm Street.
5 Walk down Elm until you see a tech store and a hair salon.
6 Walk a little more.
7 The train station will be on your right.

Pronunciation skill

Write the five vowels on the board and a selection of consonants in another group. Ask students what the two groups are, and elicit the words *consonant* and *vowel*. Write the four sentences from the *Linking sounds* box on the board. Say the sentences aloud to students and then drill them on their pronunciation, focusing on the linking of the sounds.

1 Write the first sentence on the board and mark the linking sounds. Ask students to mark the rest of the linking sounds and compare with a partner.

ANSWERS

1 It's_on your right.
2 Walk_about ten minutes.
3 You can't miss_it.
4 Can_I help you?
5 Go to Second_Avenue.
6 Can you give me some_information?

2 Play the audio and then practice saying the sentences together as a class.

AUDIO SCRIPT 2.13

1 It's on your right.
2 Walk about ten minutes.
3 You can't miss it.
4 Can I help you?
5 Go to Second Avenue.
6 Can you give me some information?

Ask students to write three sentences containing linking sounds. Students should then give their sentences to a partner who should try to say them aloud. Ask one or two pairs to say their sentences for the whole class.

3 After students have practiced this activity in pairs, ask one or two students to practice the pronunciation in front of the class.

SPEAKING TASK

Before asking students to read the conversation and do the task, elicit what students can see in the picture. Ask them if they have anything like that in their neighborhood and if so, what games they like to play.

ANSWERS

A: Do you ever go to the video arcade in this neighborhood?
B: No.
A: It's a cool place. You <u>can</u> play some really fun games there. You <u>can</u> also get food and drinks if you want.
B: Really? Where is it exactly? <u>Can</u> you give me directions?
A: Sure. First, walk down the small street by our school. Follow it for about ten minutes. Then turn right at the big tech store. Do you know the one?
B: Yeah.
A: After that, walk about two more minutes. You will see a small street on the left. Go down that street until you see the arcade. It's on the first floor. You <u>can't</u> miss it.
B: Great! I <u>can't</u> wait to go.

Brainstorm

1 Ask students to work individually to make notes about a interesting place near the school.

2 As an example, pick a place near the school. On the board, write down three things you can do there and ask students to guess the place. Draw a simple map on the board and put an *X* where the school is. Ask one student to come to the board. Give directions on how to get to the place and have the student draw the route on the map. Another alternative for technology-enabled classes is to display a Google Map or a Google Earth image and look at how to go from one place to another through the *Get directions* function.

Plan

Encourage students to write out the directions and to think about when they will need to link sounds together.

Speak and share

Have students ask their partners about the place they have written about. They should also ask how to get there. When pairs have practiced their conversations, invite one pair of volunteers to present one of theirs to the class.

Put students into groups to do the *Share* task. If you have the technology, you could project a map of the area around your school onto the screen. Students can discuss if they agree with their classmates' directions. During this stage, monitor and take language notes. Use the photocopiable *Unit assignment checklist* on page 94 to assess the students' speaking.

STUDY SKILLS Current skills and qualities

In order for students to develop better study skills, it is a good idea to identify their weaker areas. These weak areas can then be developed. It might be difficult to ask people to identify their weak points, as they might not know where to start. A survey or checklist of skills can provide an easy way to assess where weaknesses might be. The items on this particular checklist mainly relate to personal qualities. Developing E.Q. (emotional quotient) is just as important as developing I.Q. (intelligence quotient) in many academic cultures.

In some cases, it is not culturally appropriate to admit to weak points. Establishing a person's strengths before their weak points can also foster a sense of confidence in acknowledging that he/she already has a set of solid skills and qualities to work from. The person shouldn't feel like a "failure."

Get the students to go through each item in the checklist. They should put a check mark alongside the items they are good at. They should mark the items that they are really good at with a star. Be aware that some students might feel self-conscious to share their list with another person. Emphasize that this is a personal list, for which there are no right or wrong answers. You can also display your own list as a model for the students.

There may be some words in the checklist that the students don't know. Some of these words might need to be pre-taught and might include: *negotiating, take instruction, priorities, coping, determination and perseverance, motivating.*

As an extension, students could mark the other checklist items with other symbols. They could use an unhappy face for items they don't feel confident in. They could mark items that they feel they really find difficult with an exclamation point, and so on.

When the checklist is complete, students should be told to display their list in a private place at home. They should remember that they do have lots of skills. They should also think about ways they can improve on things they are not so good at.

Listening	Listening to confirm predictions
Vocabulary	Recognizing homophones
Grammar	*So* and *neither*
Pronunciation	Stress in responses
Speaking	Expressing likes and dislikes

Discussion point

Ask students to look at the picture on page 77 and ask who might like to watch this TV program.

Ask students to discuss the questions with a partner, using the sentence frames to help them get started. Photocopy and cut out the *Useful language* on page 84 to provide some extra support. After they have discussed the questions, ask one or two students to share their answers with the class. You could extend this activity by identifying the adjectives from the *Useful language* page, and asking students to divide them into positive and negative adjectives. Then ask students to add one or two more words to each column.

Cultural awareness

The popularity of sports around the world varies greatly. Soccer (called football in the U.K.) is popular in many countries. In the U.S., American football is much more popular than soccer. However, outside of the U.S. very few countries play the sport. Other sports that are popular with a limited number of countries include rugby and cricket. Cricket is incredibly popular in India and Pakistan. Baseball is popular in the U.S. and Japan. Basketball is very popular in the U.S. and is growing in popularity in countries such as China.

Vocabulary preview 1

1 Before students match the show types with the definitions, you might need to pre-teach some of the vocabulary in the definitions, such as *serious, prize, host, interview, character*.

```
ANSWERS
1 c    3 a    5 d    7 h    9 g
2 b    4 f    6 e    8 i
```

2 Ask students to discuss these questions in pairs and then report back some of their answers to the class. Extend the discussion by asking students these questions: *Which three types of show are your favorites? Why do you like those types of show? What's your favorite show in each category?*

LISTENING 1 I miss that show!

Before you listen

Ask students to close their books. Then, write the following sentence on the board:

The average American or British adult spends nine years _____ before the age of 65.

Elicit what they think might go in the blank. If students are struggling for ideas, give them the following suggestions: *sleeping, going to school, eating, driving, watching TV, surfing the Internet.* After discussing their answers, have the students open their books and work with a partner to discuss the questions.

Global listening

Before playing the audio, write the following on the board: *Ahmed is from Saudi Arabia. Now he is living in the USA. He misses …* Ask students what they think Ahmed misses. Change the country and name to one that best suits your situation if necessary. Then play the audio and have students match the person to the type of show.

AUDIO SCRIPT 2.14
Peter: Hi, Les. What are you watching?
Les: Oh, it's a soap opera.
Peter: You like soap operas?
Les: Not really. This one just reminds me of a soap opera from my country called *Generations*. I kind of miss it.
Peter: *Generations*. Never heard of it. Is it a new show?
Les: No, not at all. It started in 1994. It's still on.
Peter: I think you're a little homesick.
Les: Yes, I think I am. What show do you like, Peter?
Peter: There's a documentary series I really like.
Les: What's it called?
Peter: *Nature*. It's a long-running show. It started in 1982, and it's still on. The show talks about animals and natural history. I like it because I'm a Biology major, so it's been helpful for my studies. Actually, my teachers sometimes showed the documentary in class.
Les: Do you watch it now?
Peter: I don't really have time, but I watch it online sometimes.
David: Hey, guys. How's it going?
Peter: Hi, David. Les and I are just talking about TV shows we miss. What are some good shows from your country?
David: TV shows? I don't watch TV much. But I did like *Bondi Rescue*. That was good.
Les: *Bondi Rescue*?

David: Yeah, It's a reality show, I guess. They film it at Bondi Beach in Sydney. That's a famous beach with locals and tourists. My old high school is near there. I always go when I go back and see my parents. The show is about lifeguards—they save lives. It's pretty exciting.

Feng: Did I hear someone mention *Bondi Rescue*?

David: Oh, hi, Feng. Yeah, *Bondi Rescue* is a show from Australia.

Feng: I love that show. I've seen it here. They show it on channel 43.

David: They do? Great! I didn't know that.

Peter: Do you miss any TV shows from Singapore?

Feng: Um, yeah. I miss this show called *Under One Roof*.

Les: Is that a reality show?

Feng: No, it's a sitcom. It isn't on anymore, though. I have a lot of the episodes on DVD, but I don't have them here. They're all at home. I miss them!

ANSWERS

1 b   2 d   3 a   4 c

Close listening

1   Before playing the audio, ask students to read the sentences and answer any they can remember.

Exam tip

True, False, and *Not given* is a common question type in the IELTS Test. Simple true and false questions such as these are good practice for lower level students. Students should look for key words to narrow down the language area in a text that they need to focus on. Students should re-read the information in order to determine if they really do have enough information to confirm true or false, or whether not enough information is given.

AUDIO SCRIPT   2.15

Peter: Hi, Les. What are you watching?

Les: Oh, it's a soap opera.

Peter: You like soap operas?

Les: Not really. This one just reminds me of a soap opera from my country called *Generations*. I kind of miss it.

Peter: *Generations*. Never heard of it. Is it a new show?

Les: No, not at all. It started in 1994. It's still on.

Peter: I think you're a little homesick.

Les: Yes, I think I am. What show do you like, Peter?

Peter: There's a documentary series I really like.

Les: What's it called?

Peter: *Nature*. It's a long-running show. It started in 1982, and it's still on. The show talks about animals and natural history. I like it because I'm a Biology major, so it's been helpful for my studies. Actually, my teachers sometimes showed the documentary in class.

Les: Do you watch it now?

Peter: I don't really have time, but I watch it online sometimes.

ANSWERS

1 F   2 T   3 F   4 T   5 F   6 T

---

2   Check that students can remember what *infer* means (to guess, using clues to help). Then play the audio and ask students to do the task.

AUDIO SCRIPT   2.16

David: Hey, guys. How's it going?

Peter: Hi, David. Les and I are just talking about TV shows we miss. What are some good shows from your country?

David: TV shows? I don't watch TV much. But I did like *Bondi Rescue*. That was good.

Les: *Bondi Rescue*?

David: Yeah, It's a reality show, I guess. They film it at Bondi Beach in Sydney. That's a famous beach with locals and tourists. My old high school is near there. I always go when I go back and see my parents. The show is about lifeguards—they save lives. It's pretty exciting.

Feng: Did I hear someone mention *Bondi Rescue*?

David: Oh, hi, Feng. Yeah, *Bondi Rescue* is a show from Australia.

Feng: I love that show. I've seen it here. They show it on channel 43.

David: They do? Great! I didn't know that.

Peter: Do you miss any TV shows from Singapore?

Feng: Um, yeah. I miss this show called *Under One Roof*.

Les: Is that a reality show?

Feng: No, it's a sitcom. It isn't on anymore, though. I have a lot of the episodes on DVD, but I don't have them here. They're all at home. I miss them!

ANSWERS

1 –   2 ✓   3 –   4 ✓   5 ✓   6 –

Over to you

Before asking students to discuss the questions in groups, have them write down a few shows they watched when they were nine or ten, and a few shows they watched recently that are not on TV anymore. Refer students to the *Possible reasons* box for ideas.

Vocabulary preview 2

1 If possible, bring in pictures or find some on the Internet to help students understand the vocabulary. Alternatively, write example sentences on the board to give more context. For example, write: *We have three bins in the classroom: one for paper, one for pens, one for language magazines.*

ANSWERS

1 c 2 d 3 a 4 b 5 e 6 h 7 f 8 g

2 Have students complete the sentences individually and then check their answers in pairs.

ANSWERS

1 garbage	5 escalator
2 arcade	6 deep
3 bin	7 fall
4 experiment	8 theory

3 Ask and answer the first question with a student. Then have students ask and answer the rest in pairs, and have them report back to the class anything interesting their partner said.

LISTENING 2 The fun theory

Before you listen

Background information

The fun theory is based on a real competition to display creative ideas based on the notion of making ordinary events fun. The competition was initiated by Volkswagen, and competition entries can be viewed online via: http://www.thefuntheory.com/.

You might want to give students a few ideas to help them with this task. Write the following on the board, and ask students to divide them into things they like doing and things they don't like doing: *cooking, cleaning, dusting, shopping, playing sports, walking, doing homework, surfing the web, chatting on the phone.*

After you have done this, ask students to tell their partner why they don't like doing each task.

Global listening

1 After playing the audio, ask students to predict what they think will happen in the experiments.

AUDIO SCRIPT 2.17

Good morning class. Are we ready to begin? I want to talk today about three interesting ads and an idea about how we behave. A Swedish company created these ads for the German car company Volkswagen. In these ads, Volkswagen asks the question "Can you change people's

behavior by making things more fun?" What do you think? The answer is yes. They call this "The fun theory." Let's look at the three experiments that featured in the ads.

ANSWER

You can change people's behavior by making things more fun.

2 After students have listened to the audio and numbered the pictures, elicit which experiment they think is the most interesting and why.

AUDIO SCRIPT 2.18

The first experiment is called "Piano Stairs." We often hear it's better to take the stairs, right? They're healthier than riding an escalator or an elevator. But how many of us do that? Raise your hands. Oh, not many at all. Well, in a subway station, they have an escalator, and next to it some stairs. The experimenters decide to make the stairs more fun. How exactly? Well, the stairs look like a piano, and they play music when you walk up and down them. Fun, right? What percentage of the people take the "Piano Stairs"? What do you think?

The second experiment is called "Bottle Bank Arcade." Many of us return cans and plastic bottles. People often do this because they get money back. In some places, however, they don't get money for returning glass bottles. Researchers found that fewer people return these bottles. Not so good for the environment. So, how can we make returning bottles more fun? Make it like a game. It works like this. First, you press start and wait for the light. Then you put the bottle in. Finally, you get points for each bottle. The bottle bank lights up and makes noise, just like a video game in an arcade. In one evening, just two people use a regular bin nearby. How many people use the "Bottle Bank Arcade" on one evening?

The third experiment is called "The World's Deepest Bin." Most of us put our garbage in the garbage can. We don't throw it on the ground. But some people do. How do we get them to put their garbage in the garbage can? Yes, as before, we make it fun! When people put garbage in this can, it sounds like it falls about 20 meters. It sounds something like this. A normal can in a park receives 31 kilograms of garbage each day. So, researchers wanted to know how much garbage "The World's Deepest Bin" gets. Can you guess how much?

ANSWERS

1 b 2 c 3 a

Close listening

1 Play the complete audio and ask students to circle the correct answers.

AUDIO SCRIPT 2.19

Good morning, class. Are we ready to begin? I want to talk today about three interesting ads and an idea about how we behave. A Swedish company created these ads for the German car company Volkswagen. In these ads, Volkswagen asks the question "Can you change people's behavior by making things more fun?" What do you think? The answer is yes. They call this "The fun theory." Let's look at the three experiments that featured in the ads.

The first experiment is called "Piano Stairs." We often hear it's better to take the stairs, right? They're healthier than riding an escalator or an elevator. But how many of us do that? Raise your hands? Oh, not many at all. Well, in a subway station, they have an escalator, and next to it some stairs. The experimenters decided to make the stairs more fun. How exactly? Well, the stairs look like a piano, and they play music when you walk up and down them. Fun, right? What percentage of the people take the "Piano Stairs"? What do you think?

The second experiment is called "Bottle Bank Arcade." Many of us return cans and plastic bottles. People often do this because they get money back. In some places, however, they don't get money for returning glass bottles. Researchers found that fewer people return these bottles. Not so good for the environment. So, how can we make returning bottles more fun? Make it like a game. It works like this. First, you press start and wait for the light. Then you put the bottle in. Finally, you get points for each bottle. The bottle bank lights up and makes noise, just like a video game in an arcade. In one evening, just two people use a regular bin nearby. How many people use the "Bottle Bank Arcade" on one evening?

The third experiment is called "The World's Deepest Bin." Most of us put our garbage in the garbage can. We don't throw it on the ground. But some people do. How do we get them to put their garbage in the garbage can? Yes, as before, we make it fun! When people put garbage in this can, it sounds like it falls about 20 meters. It sounds something like this … A normal can in a park receives 31 kilograms of garbage each day. So, researchers wanted to know how much garbage "The World's Deepest Bin" gets. Can you guess how much?

ANSWERS

1	Swedish	4	points
2	Not many	5	20
3	glass	6	in a park

Ask students to read the *Listening to confirm predictions* box. Explain to them that the more they know about a topic, the easier it is to understand a text they are listening to. Knowing even just a little bit about a topic can help in making simple predictions.

2 After students have made their predictions, invite volunteers to explain the reason for their choices.

3 After students have listened to the full lecture and checked their answers, look back at the numbers and practice saying them as a class. Then ask students to write down another percentage, whole number, and weight. Students then dictate their numbers to a partner, who then writes them down.

AUDIO SCRIPT 2.20

The first experiment is called "Piano Stairs." We often hear it's better to take the stairs, right? They're healthier than riding an escalator or an elevator. But how many of us do that? Raise your hands? Oh, not many at all. Well, in a subway station, they have an escalator, and next to it some stairs. The experimenters decided to make the stairs more fun. How exactly? Well, the stairs look like a piano, and they play music when you walk up and down them. Fun, right? What percentage of the people take the "Piano Stairs"? What do you think? Results showed 66% more than normal. That's a big increase.

The second experiment is called "Bottle Bank Arcade." Many of us return cans and plastic bottles. People often do this because they get money back. In some places, however, they don't get money for returning glass bottles. Researchers found that fewer people return these bottles. Not so good for the environment. So, how can we make returning bottles more fun? Make it like a game. It works like this. First, you press start and wait for the light. Then you put the bottle in. Finally, you get points for each bottle. The bottle bank lights up and makes noise, just like a video game in an arcade. In one evening, just two people use a regular bin nearby. How many people use the "Bottle Bank Arcade" on one evening? Over one hundred people. Amazing, huh?

The third experiment is called "The World's Deepest Bin." Most of us put our garbage in the garbage can. We don't throw it on the ground. But some people do. How do we get them to put their garbage in the garbage can? Yes, as before, we make it fun! When people put garbage in this can, it sounds like it falls about 20 meters. It sounds something like this … A normal can in a park receives 31 kilograms of garbage each day. So, researchers wanted to know how much garbage "The World's Deepest Bin" gets. Can you guess how much? Every day it gets 72 kilograms. That's 41 kilograms more than normal.

ANSWERS
1 c   2 b   3 b

Over to you

After students have discussed the questions in groups, invite volunteers to report back some of their ideas to the class.

Vocabulary skill

Before asking students to read the *Recognizing homophones* box, say the following words aloud and ask students to write down what they hear: *write, sell, I*. After they have read the box, have students write down homophones for the words you dictated. Possible answers could be: *right, cell/sale/sail, eye*.

1 Ask students to correct the sentences individually. Then check the answers with the class.

> **ANSWERS**
> 1 A polar ~~bare~~ **bear** spends some of its life on the ice.
> 2 Walk ~~threw~~ **through** the park, and then take a right.
> 3 You can ~~by~~ **buy** four tickets for a dollar at the video arcade.
> 4 Let's ~~meat~~ **meet** by the escalator inside the main doors of the mall.
> 5 Hurry to the department store because everything is on ~~sail~~ **sale**.
> 6 The new ~~rode~~ **road** to my high school is blocked by snow today.

2 Quickly check that students understand the words in the box before asking them to complete the sentences.

> **ANSWERS**
> 1 hi; high   5 eight; ate
> 2 guest; guessed   6 here; hear
> 3 add; ad   7 wait; weight
> 4 there; their   8 right; write

3 After students have worked in pairs, invite volunteers to share their sentences with the class.

SPEAKING Discussing likes and dislikes

This is a good place to use the video resource *Time for vacation!* It is located in the Video resources section of the digital component. Alternatively, remind the students about the video resource so they can do this at home.

Grammar

Write the following sentences on the board: *Colin is late, and _____ is Paul. Mohammed isn't here, and _____ is Ahmed.* Elicit what words go in the blanks. If students have no idea, write *so* and *neither* on the board, and ask which one goes in which blank. Then ask the students to read the *Grammar* box.

1 Ask students to work out which sentences will be followed by *so* and which ones will be followed by *neither*. Then play the audio.

> **AUDIO SCRIPT 2.21**
> 1 Nadia is online, and so is Susan.
> 2 My classmates enjoy this class, and so do I.
> 3 I like game shows, and so does my husband.

> 4 I'm not a fan of reality shows, and neither are my friends.
> 5 Haley doesn't go out much, and neither do her sisters.
> 6 I don't watch much TV, and neither does my best friend.

> **ANSWERS**
> 1 so is Susan
> 2 so do I
> 3 so does my husband
> 4 neither are my friends
> 5 neither do her sisters
> 6 neither does my best friend

2 Before having students circle the verbs, review the correct forms of *be* and *do* for each pronoun on the board.

> **ANSWERS**
> 1 does   2 do   3 am   4 is   5 are   6 do

3 After students have completed the sentences with a partner, ask them to write one more sentence with *so* and another with *neither*. Invite volunteers to each read their sentences to the class.

Speaking skill

Before asking students to read the *Expressing likes and dislikes* box, write the following on the board: *like, hate, like a lot, don't like very much, don't like, love*. Ask students to put them in order from the weakest to the strongest feeling.

1 Have students compare their answers in pairs before checking the answers together as a class.

> **ANSWERS**
> 1 Luke likes reality shows a lot.
> 2 I don't like sitcoms at all.
> 3 I hate watching game shows.
> 4 Rex doesn't like watching TV very much.
> 5 Shannon loves to download TV shows.
> 6 I like reading novels very much.

2 Have students write sentences and then discuss them with a partner. Tell students they should ask their partner at least one follow-up question for each statement, e.g., *What sports do you like to watch?*

Pronunciation skill

Ask a volunteer to read out one of their sentences about something they like from the *Speaking skill* section. Respond with *So do I*, using the correct stress. Have another volunteer read out one of the things they don't like. Respond with *Neither do I*, using the correct stress. Elicit if students noticed your pronunciation and stress patterns. If they haven't, repeat the two answers.

Then have them read the *Stress in responses* box.

1 Have students underline the stressed words before you play the audio to check their answers. After you have checked the answers, have students practice saying the sentences with a partner.

AUDIO SCRIPT 2.22

1

A: I don't like dramas at all.

B: Really? I do.

2

A: I love to read short stories.

B: So do I.

3

A: I don't like to stay out late.

B: Neither do I.

4

A: I like to play chess.

B: Oh? I don't.

ANSWERS

1 Really? I do.   3 Neither do I.

2 So do I.   4 Oh? I don't.

---

2 After students have read their sentences and responded in pairs, invite volunteers to model their sentences for the class.

SPEAKING TASK

Before asking students to read the discussion individually, invite three students to read it aloud. Make sure students focus on their stress in the responses.

ANSWERS

A: Let's watch TV. Sound good?

B: Sure. What do you want to watch?

A: How about Sunday Nights Sports? I love that show.

B: Really? I don't. I find it boring. But I love to watch soccer.

A: So do I. But there's no soccer on—just baseball.

C: Life with Mickey is on. I like that show.

A: Oh? I don't. I don't find it funny at all. But I like that reality show Super Student.

C: So do I.

B: Can we watch a documentary? I see that Extreme Journeys is on. I love that show.

C: I don't like it at all. Sorry.

A: Neither do I.

B: It's not easy to agree on anything.

C: Why don't we go outside and do something? We can go to the park.

Brainstorm and plan

To introduce the *Brainstorm* activity, you could write the chart on the board and elicit one item for each cell from different students in the class.

Ask students to look at their chart in the *Brainstorm* activity and rank their likes and dislikes. Have students explain their rankings.

Speak and share

The *Speak* activity should be done in a small group. Monitor and help students with any stress problems.

For the *Share* activity, make sure students work with a partner who was in a different group. During this stage, monitor and take language notes. Use the photocopiable *Unit assignment checklist* on page 95 to assess the students' speaking.

STUDY SKILLS Prioritizing tasks

Getting started

Before students make their own lists, generate a whole-class discussion on different things people have to do in their everyday lives.

Scenario

Give students time to read the scenario and make suggestions for Ling. Help students with any problem words. Have a whole-class discussion to share ideas.

POSSIBLE ANSWER

Ling is doing a number of things correctly. Firstly, she is making a list of things to do. She is also prioritizing her tasks and thinking about deadlines. Unfortunately, she does not think carefully about how long each task will take and so does not have enough time. Additionally, it is a mistake to do the easy things first. She should make the important things a priority.

Consider it

Ask students to discuss the tips in pairs. If students disagree with any of the tips, ask them to explain why.

Over to you

After students have completed the activity and compared their lists, invite one or two volunteers to tell the class about their list.

Extra research task

Ask students to keep track of their prioritizing list and in one or two weeks' time, ask them to report back on their progress.

UNIT 9 PLANS

Listening	Listening for reasons
Vocabulary	Forming compound nouns
Grammar	Verb + infinitive
Pronunciation	Reduction of *have to*
Speaking	Making, accepting, and declining invitations

Discussion point

Ask students to look at the picture on page 87 and generate a discussion based on these questions: *What can you see in the picture? Why do you think the person has written all of these things down? How do you remember to do things? What else can you use sticky notes for?*

For the last question, you could suggest to students that sticky notes make good revision aids. Vocabulary can be written on the notes and placed around a room so that students see them while they go about their normal day.

Ask students to discuss the questions with a partner, using the prompts to help them get started. Photocopy and cut out the *Useful language* on pages 85 and 86 to provide some extra support. (There are two *Useful language* pages in this unit, one for each of the *Discussion point* questions.) After they have discussed the questions, ask volunteers to report their partner's answers to the class.

This is a good place to use the video resource *Career choices*. It is located in the Video resources section of the digital component. Alternatively, remind students about the video resource so they can do this at home.

Cultural awareness

Countries can be divided into monochronic and polychronic depending on their attitude to time. Monochronic cultures, such as much of northern Europe, tend to place great importance on the clock and being punctual. Therefore, planning is essential. Expressions in these countries, such as "time is money" and "time waits for no man," show a lot about attitudes towards time. In polychronic cultures, the event and the people are more important than the clock. People are more willing to have a more flexible approach to time. Of course, individuals in all of these cultures will be different, but it might be worth discussing briefly with your students.

Vocabulary preview 1

1 Before asking students to do the task, write the verbs from the first column on the board. Ask students to think of a possible word that goes with each. Give the first one as an example.

ANSWERS
1 b   2 c   3 a   4 d   5 c   6 d   7 c   8 b

2 Encourage students to give reasons for their preferences. After students have worked with their partner, have them report why their partner prefers to do an activity alone or with someone else.

LISTENING 1 My plans

Before you listen

1 When students have done this exercise individually and then compared answers with their partner, say the following sentences aloud and ask students to write down which day or month it is that you are going to do these things:

Today is Friday. I'm going to my parents' house the day after tomorrow.

It's January. Next month, I'm going to Madrid.

It's Thursday. Tomorrow afternoon, I'm going shopping.

ANSWERS
1 tonight
2 tomorrow morning
3 tomorrow afternoon
4 tomorrow night
5 the day after tomorrow
6 this weekend
7 next weekend
8 next month

2 Remind students to use the time expressions from exercise 1 and the activities from *Vocabulary preview 1* to talk about their plans.

Global listening

Generate a discussion about what the students see in the pictures. Then play the audio and ask students to check or cross the pictures.

AUDIO SCRIPT 2.23
Michelle: I have a busy few days ahead of me. First, tonight I'm planning to go bowling with my friends Wendy and Sarah. Then on Saturday morning, I'm going to visit my parents. They live about 200 kilometers away now, and I visit them once a month or so. On Sunday afternoon at two, I'm going to play tennis with my friend Lisa. She's a good friend, but a terrible tennis player, so I usually win. Then in the evening, I plan to relax and watch a movie at home. That sounds like a nice weekend to me!

Jasper: I can't believe this day is finished—at last! Tonight at seven, I'm going to meet my friend Jeff to have dinner. He's going to cook at his place, so I'm going there. After dinner, we're planning to watch a baseball game on his new TV. The game starts at eight. Then tomorrow afternoon, I'm going to the mall to do some shopping. I need a new winter coat because the day after tomorrow I'm going to go skiing with my cousin Eddie. I'm not a very good skier, but I can't wait to be in the mountains.

Ashley: My sister is coming to visit me tomorrow. I have a lot of plans for the two of us. Tomorrow night, we're going to visit a museum. She loves art, so I want to take her to the new modern art museum. Then on Saturday afternoon, we're going to go for a drive—probably by the sea. Then that night, at eight, we're going to go to a barbecue at my friend Jessica's. My sister knows Jessica, so that will be fun. Let's see … what do I have for next week? Oh, right, on Tuesday, we're going to go hiking. I have the day off from work so the trails won't be crowded.

Saito: Why aren't there more hours in a day? I have a lot to do today. My parents and grandmother are coming over for dinner tonight, and I'm going to cook. I'm going to prepare a barbecue. I have nothing in the house, so first I need to go shopping for groceries. The store opens today at ten, so I'm going to be there when they open. After I do that, I'm going to go home and clean the house. It's a mess right now. At 2:45, I need to leave for my Spanish class. It's our last class, so I can't miss it. I get home at 5:30, so I can make dinner then. I can't wait to see everyone!

> **ANSWERS**
> Michelle ✗
> Jasper ✓
> Ashley ✓
> Saito ✗

Close listening

1 Before asking students to listen to the audio again, ask them to work with a partner and try to recall the activities each person in the audio plans to do.

> **ANSWERS**
>
> | **Michelle** | **Ashley** |
> |---|---|
> | 1 bowling | 1 museum |
> | 2 parents | 2 drive |
> | 3 tennis | 3 barbecue |
> | 4 movie | 4 hiking |
> | **Jasper** | **Saito** |
> | 1 dinner | 1 shopping |
> | 2 baseball | 2 house |
> | 3 mall | 3 Spanish |
> | 4 skiing | 4 dinner |

2 Read some of the times from the audio aloud and ask students to write down what they hear. Use a range that includes similar times said in a different way, such as *two forty five, a quarter to three,* etc. Then play the audio and ask students to write the times.

> **AUDIO SCRIPT 2.24**
> **Michelle:** I have a busy few days ahead of me. First, tonight I'm planning to go bowling with my friends Wendy and Sarah. Then on Saturday morning, I'm going to visit my parents.
>
> **Jasper:** I can't believe this day is finished—at last! Tonight at seven, I'm going to meet my friend Jeff for dinner. He's going to cook at his place, so I'm going there.
>
> **Ashley:** My sister is coming to visit me tomorrow. I have a lot of plans for the two of us. Tomorrow night, we're going to visit a museum. She loves art, so I want to take her to the new modern art museum.
>
> **Saito:** At 2:45, I need to leave for my Spanish class. It's our last class, so I can't miss it. I get home at 5:30, so I can make dinner then. I can't wait to see everyone!

> **ANSWERS**
> 1 tonight
> 2 tonight at seven
> 3 tomorrow night
> 4 at 2:45

Over to you

To help generate the discussions between groups, give them a range of people they might possibly have plans with, e.g., classmates, friends, parents, etc.

Vocabulary preview 2

1 After students have matched each chore to a picture, have them rank the chores from most to least favorite. When they have done this individually, ask them to compare their ideas with a partner and to give reasons for their choices.

> **ANSWERS**
>
> | 1 wash the dishes | 5 water the plants |
> |---|---|
> | 2 do the laundry | 6 clean the house |
> | 3 Buy groceries | 7 pay the bills |
> | 4 take out the garbage | 8 put away the groceries |

2 If students have left home and no longer live with their parents, you could also ask them about how they feel about having to do more chores.

LISTENING 2 Are you free?

Before you listen

1 Before asking students to discuss the excuses with a partner, generate a discussion about some situations in which they might want to make excuses. For example:

Your grandmother invites you over for lunch, but she always tells the same stories, and you saw her last week.

Your friend wants to watch a movie that you think will be really boring.

Your boss wants you to work late, but you have plans.

2 Do this task as a whole class. Encourage students to give you excuses they have used in the past. Expand this into a discussion about excuses they could give that would not upset the other person.

Global listening

Before playing the audio, ask students to predict what the callers might suggest doing and in what location. For example, *study → library*. Then ask students to listen and check the correct answers.

AUDIO SCRIPT 2.25

1

Mike: Hello.

Josh: Hi, Mike? It's Josh. How's it going?

Mike: Oh, pretty good. What's up?

Josh: Our study group is meeting at the library at seven o'clock. We're going to go over our notes from today's lecture. Do you want to join us?

Mike: Tonight?

Josh: Yeah.

Mike: I'd love to, but I can't. I need to do the laundry tonight.

Josh: Oh, well, that's OK.

Mike: Thanks, though. See you in class on Monday.

2

Suzie: Hello.

Celia: Suzie?

Suzie: Yeah.

Celia: It's Celia. Are you free?

Suzie: Sure. I'm just doing my homework.

Celia: Yeah, me too, but I need a break. Do you want to go bowling? I'm meeting my friend Julia at The Downtown Lanes at 7:30.

Suzie: At 7:30? Um, sure, I'd love to go.

Celia: Can you meet us there?

Suzie: Sure. Can I bring a friend, too?

Celia: Of course! That's a great idea.

Suzie: OK, I'll call my friend Ruby. She loves to bowl.

3

Kyle: Hello.

Dan: Kyle?

Kyle: Yeah.

Dan: It's me, Dan. What are you doing?

Kyle: Nothing much, just watching a baseball game on TV.

Dan: There is a free talk at the bookstore tonight. A professor is going to talk about her research in Africa. Do you want to meet me there, say around 6:45?

Kyle: Sorry, I can't.

Dan: Oh?

Kyle: Yeah, I have to clean the house.

Dan: That doesn't sound fun.

Kyle: Tell me about it.

4

Dana: Hello. First Street Café.

Alice: Dana?

Dana: Yes.

Alice: It's Alice. I'm sorry to call you at work. Are you free?

Dana: Um, sure.

Alice: Great. Listen, do you want to plan our group project tomorrow?

Dana: Sure. I'd love to. I have some great ideas to share.

Alice: Oh good. I already talked to Carrie, and she can make it.

Dana: Great. But listen, I need to run. Call me tomorrow with more details.

Alice: OK.

5

Ben: Hello.

Dave: Is Ben there?

Ben: This is Ben.

Dave: Oh, sorry. This is Dave ... from our painting class.

Ben: Oh, right, Dave. How are you?

Dave: Pretty good. Listen, do you know the Madison Art Museum?

Ben: Of course.

Dave: There's a Picasso exhibit there, and it's ending tomorrow. Would you like to see it with me? I know how much you like Picasso.

Ben: I'd really like to, but I can't. Sorry. I have to study for a test.

Dave: Oh, that's too bad.

Ben: Sorry.

Dave: Oh that's OK.

ANSWERS
1 join a study group
2 go bowling
3 attend a talk
4 plan a project
5 visit a museum

Close listening

1 Before playing the audio again, check students know the meaning of *accept* and *decline*. After playing the audio and checking the answers, ask students to read the *Listening for reasons* box.

ANSWERS
1 decline
2 accept
3 decline
4 accept
5 decline

2 Before playing the excerpts, ask students to discuss with a partner whether they can remember the reason given. Then play the audio and have students write the reasons. Check the answers with the class.

AUDIO SCRIPT   2.26
1
Josh: Our study group is meeting at the library at seven o'clock. We're going to go over our notes from today's lecture. Do you want to join us?
Mike: Tonight?
Josh: Yeah.
Mike: I'd love to, but I can't. I need to do the laundry tonight.
2
Dan: There is a free talk at the bookstore tonight. A professor is going to talk about her research in Africa. Do you want to meet me there, say around 6:45?
Kyle: Sorry, I can't.
Dan: Oh?
Kyle: Yeah, I have to clean the house.
3
Dave: Pretty good. Listen, do you know the Madison Art Museum?
Ben: Of course.
Dave: There's a Picasso exhibit there, and it's ending tomorrow. Would you like to see it with me? I know how much you like Picasso.
Ben: I'd really like to, but I can't. Sorry. I have to study for a test.
Dave: Oh, that's too bad.

ANSWERS
1 I need to do the laundry tonight.
2 I have to clean the house.
3 I have to study for a test.

Over to you

After students have discussed these questions, ask groups to report back. Try to encourage students to give reasons each time. Remind students that the reasons may depend on who is being invited.

Vocabulary skill

1 Before asking students to read the *Forming compound nouns* box, write the following words on the board: *alarm, switch, train, clock, light, station.*

Ask students to match the pairs to make compound nouns (*alarm clock, light switch, train station*). After students have read the box, have them make the compound nouns in exercise 1.

ANSWERS
1 movie theater
2 hair salon
3 stationery store
4 graduation dinner
5 tennis player
6 video arcade
7 bus station
8 amusement park

2 Before asking students to complete the puzzle, explain that the words in the blanks make compound nouns with the words before them.

ANSWERS

		¹M	U	S	E	U	²M		
		A					A		
	³P	A	R	T	Y		L		
		K			⁴B	A	L	L	
		E							
	⁵S	T	A	T	I	⁶O	N		
		T				F			
⁷S	T	O	P			F			
		R				I			
		E				C			
			⁸G	A	M	E			

3 Invite volunteers to model the example in the book for the rest of the class. Then have students play the game in groups.

SPEAKING Inviting people to do things with you

Grammar

Before asking students to read the *Grammar* box, write these two sentences on the board:

I want ___ go shopping. I need ___ buy a new tablet.

Elicit from students what one word goes in both blanks. Ask students to read the *Grammar* box.

1 Remind students they need to focus more on the meaning of the verbs in the box rather than on the grammatical structure. Have them complete the sentences, then check the answers with the class.

> **ANSWERS**
> 1 to wash
> 2 to see
> 3 to do
> 4 to go
> 5 to have
> 6 to buy
> 7 to study
> 8 to book

2 Before asking students to put the questions in order individually, write the first one on the board and do it together as a class. Then check the answers.

> **ANSWERS**
> 1 What do you plan to do this weekend?
> 2 What grade do you hope to get in this class?
> 3 Do you need to do any chores today?
> 4 Do you have to study this evening?
> 5 Where would you like to travel someday?

3 After students have asked and answered the questions, invite volunteers to report back to the class about their partner's answers.

Pronunciation skill

Before asking students to read the *Reduction of have to* box, write the phrase *have to* on the board and ask students to pronounce it aloud. Model both forms for students and drill them on the reduced form. Tell students that there is no rule for when the reduced form is used and both are fine, but that the reduced form is very common in natural speech.

1 Play the audio twice. The first time, ask students to note what the speaker has to do. The second time, ask students to practice pronouncing the reduction of *have to*.

> **AUDIO SCRIPT 2.27**
> I have to call my parents.
> I don't have to work.
> I have to finish my homework.
> I don't have to cook dinner.

2 After students have practiced speaking with a partner, invite volunteers to speak to the class. Focus on their pronunciation of *have to* and correct where necessary.

Speaking skill

Before asking students to read the *Making, accepting, and declining invitations* box, ask the class: *Would you like to go to a movie?* Elicit some students to accept your invitation and others to decline. Then ask students to read the box and compare their responses with those in the box.

1 Have students number the parts of the conversations in pairs before playing the audio.

> **AUDIO SCRIPT 2.28**
> **Conversation 1**
> **A:** Are you free tonight?
> **B:** Yeah. I think so.
> **A:** Do you want to go see *Super Drive 3* at the Green Theater?
> **B:** Thanks. I'd love to.
> **A:** Great. Is the seven o'clock show OK?
> **B:** Sure. Let's meet at the theater.
> **Conversation 2**
> **C:** Would you like to go to a baseball game tonight?
> **D:** What time is the game?
> **C:** At seven this evening.
> **D:** Sorry, I can't. I have to meet my study group.
> **C:** That's too bad.
> **D:** Maybe some other time.

> **ANSWERS**
> **Conversation 1**
> 1 **A:** Are you free tonight?
> 2 **B:** Yeah. I think so.
> 3 **A:** Do you want to go see *Super Drive 3* at the Green Theater?
> 4 **B:** Thanks. I'd love to.
> 5 **A:** Great. Is the 7:00 show OK?
> 6 **B:** Sure. Let's meet at the theater.
> **Conversation 2**
> 1 **A:** Would you like to go to a baseball game tonight?
> 2 **B:** What time is the game?
> 3 **A:** At 7:00 this evening.
> 4 **B:** Sorry, I can't. I have to meet my study group.
> 5 **A:** That's too bad.
> 6 **B:** Maybe some other time.

2 After students have practiced the conversations in pairs, ask for volunteers to act out the conversations for the class. With stronger classes, work on intonation patterns that show enthusiasm when accepting, and a rising and falling pattern when declining.

3 Encourage students to think of a wide range of excuses, and write them on the board. You could also refer them back to those used in the *Listening 2* section.

SPEAKING TASK

Ask students to read the conversations and do the task. With stronger classes, you could project the conversations on the board with the verb + infinitive phrases removed and listed separately. Then ask students to fill in the blanks.

ANSWERS

A: Are you free on Tuesday afternoon?
B: Yes, I am.
A: Do you want to work on our class project?
B: Sure. I'd love to. What time?
A: How about at 3:00?
B: That sounds good.
C: Are you busy on Saturday?
D: A little. Why?
C: Would you like to go to the museum?
D: What time?
C: At 1:30.
D: I'm sorry, but I can't. I have to study at the library then.
C: That's OK.

Brainstorm

1 Remind students to start on today's day, e.g., if today is Thursday, March 7th, they should write *March 7th* in the first row under *Thursday*. March 8th and 9th would be written in the same row, but March 10th would be under *Sunday* on the second row.

2 Tell students that if they don't have many plans, they can just make things up; you can also draw students' attention back to the box in *Speaking skill* exercise 3.

Plan

Encourage students to use their imagination to plan what they want to do.

Speak and share

For the *Speak* activity, students continue "inviting" classmates to do activities with them until they have one person for each of the activities they listed.

For the *Share* activity, ask students to discuss with their partner any excuses they made when they declined an invitation. During this stage, monitor and take language notes. Use the photocopiable *Unit assignment checklist* on page 96 to assess the students' speaking.

STUDY SKILLS Emphasis on action!

Before asking students to read the strategies, ask them to work with a partner and discuss how they like to learn. Encourage students to talk about all subjects, not just English. Encourage the students to talk about different ways they study for different subjects.

Draw students' attention to the *Inactive learning strategies (A)* and ask them to read them.

EXTENSION ACTIVITY

Write the following on the board and ask students to match each one to a picture from *Inactive learning strategies (A)*.

1 Doing things that they don't need to do. (A2)
2 Not thinking about the question carefully. (A4)
3 Writing down everything they read. (A3)
4 Not writing down important things in lectures. (A1)

Draw students' attention to the *Active learning strategies (B)* and ask them to read them. You could use this *Extension activity* to make this part more interactive.

EXTENSION ACTIVITY

Ask students to discuss the following questions with a partner.

1 Have you used any of these active learning strategies?
2 Which three do you think are the best and why?
3 Which ones will you use this week?

Extra research task

Ask students to find a study skills website. If your institution has one, you could refer students to it. Have students try to find more advice on how to study effectively and then report back to the class.

UNIT 10 CELEBRATION

Listening	Taking notes while listening
Vocabulary	Identifying word families
Grammar	Quantifiers
Pronunciation	Reduction of *of* after quantifiers
Speaking	Summarizing information

Discussion point

Elicit some holidays from the students. You might need to differentiate the word *holiday*, which includes national/public holidays and *vacation*, which refers to a period of rest from study or work when many people might chose to travel somewhere. Ask students to discuss the questions with a partner, using the sentence frames to help them get started. Photocopy and cut out the *Useful language* on page 87 to provide some extra support. After they have discussed the questions, invite volunteers to share their answers with the class.

Cultural awareness

Many holidays and festivals are connected to religion or politics. You might need to consider the sensitivity of discussing some festivals depending on the country you are working in or the students' backgrounds in the class.

This would be a good point to use the video resource *In celebration of food*. It is located in the Video resources section of the digital component. Alternatively, remind the students about the video resource so they can do this at home.

Vocabulary preview 1

1 After students have matched the words with the definitions, have them guess which holiday these words are describing. Then ask which of these words could be used to describe holidays they celebrate.

ANSWERS

1 c	6 h
2 d	7 j
3 e	8 g
4 b	9 i
5 a	10 f

2 After students have discussed the questions with a partner, invite volunteers to report back to the class on what they discussed. Generate a further discussion by talking about the kinds of food people eat on those holidays.

LISTENING 1 Thanksgiving

Before you listen

After students have described the pictures with a partner, generate a discussion about the holiday. Ask them if they have a similar festival in their country.

Global listening

Background information

Make sure that students are aware that the word *fall* when it refers to a season is the American way of saying *autumn*. According to http://hotword.dictionary.com/fall/, fall used to be called *harvest*. *Harvest* has its roots in the Old Norse word, *haust*, meaning "to gather." As many populations left their agricultural lifestyles, *harvest* was replaced by *fall* which likely has its origin in the fact that leaves fall after the summer season. Originally, English only had the words for summer and winter. The words *spring* and *fall/autumn* are more recent in the English language.

Before playing the audio, ask students to try to predict the order they think the pictures will be mentioned in. Although they are unlikely to be able to guess all of them, they should be able to predict pictures f and d will be near the start, as they show the basic information regarding the history and when the holiday happens, and this kind of information is usually near the start of a presentation.

AUDIO SCRIPT 2.29

I'd like to talk today about the holiday Thanksgiving. It is celebrated in Canada and the United States. I'm going to talk about the holiday in the U.S. only.

The holiday takes place on the fourth Thursday in November, in late fall. The holiday honors the early settlers to the New World and their feast with the Native Americans there. Why is it in the fall? Because it celebrates the autumn harvest.

The history of the holiday is interesting. Before the settlers from England arrived in North America, of course Native Americans lived there. They lived there for thousands of years and knew the area well. For example, they knew how to farm, hunt, and fish. In 1621, a group of settlers had a harvest feast with a group of Native Americans. Both groups prepared food for the feast. They also played games and danced. This was the first Thanksgiving.

This painting shows what the day was like. Their meal was meat, corn, and shellfish, such as clams, mussels, and so forth. This is very different from what most people eat today.

The modern story of Thanksgiving is also interesting. Today, it still is a day to give thanks, but not just for the harvest. Families come together.

Some people decorate their homes with symbols of the harvest, such as colored dried corn.

Most people prepare a large meal. The meal is typically potatoes, corn, pumpkin pie, cranberries, and of course, roast turkey. Doesn't that look good? In fact, Thanksgiving is sometimes called "Turkey Day."

As you can see here, after the meal, many people watch football on TV. There are several important games on this day.

To summarize, Thanksgiving is a very special holiday for North Americans. The history of the holiday was about Native Americans helping the English settlers, and giving thanks for a good harvest. Today, it's a day to give more general thanks. A lot of people enjoy the day with a large meal with their families.

Thanks for listening. Any questions?

ANSWERS
1 f   2 d   3 c   4 e   5 a   6 b

Close listening

1   Have students read the *Taking notes while listening* box before working through the abbreviations and symbols list. After they have matched the abbreviations and symbols to the words, elicit some more common abbreviations or symbols. Create a word pool on the board. Essentially, students can create their own set of abbreviations and symbols for their note taking.

ANSWERS

1 &	5 e.g.,
2 =	6 1st
3 w/	7 4th
4 b/c	8 etc.

2   Before playing the audio again, ask students to read the notes, and to try to predict what symbols and abbreviations might be used in each blank. Play the audio and ask students to complete the notes, then have them compare their answers with a partner.

ANSWERS

1 &	5 =
2 4th	6 etc.
3 b/c	7 w/
4 1st	8 e.g.,

3   Emphasize that students should answer the questions in their own words. Write the students' answers on the board and highlight any good use of synonyms students have used to paraphrase the text.

POSSIBLE ANSWERS
1   It's in fall because that's when the harvest is celebrated.
2   They knew how to farm, hunt, and fish well.
3   Their meal was meat, corn, and different types of shellfish.
4   They decorate their homes and have a large meal with their family. Sometimes they watch football games on TV.

Over to you

Have students discuss the questions in groups. Continue the discussion by asking them to compare which features of Thanksgiving are similar to holidays in their own country.

Vocabulary preview 2

1   Have students circle the answers individually. They should not use dictionaries but should guess the meaning from the context.

EXTENSION ACTIVITY

For further practice, ask students to write sentences using some of the vocabulary words. For example: *A black cat symbolizes bad luck in some cultures.*

Cultural awareness

In sentence 8, the color green is used to symbolize peace, but green might not be recognized as a symbol of peace in all countries. If you are in a multicultural class, it could be interesting to discuss what different colors symbolize in each of the students' countries and compare them.

ANSWERS
1 b   2 a   3 a   4 b   5 a   6 b   7 a   8 a

2   Encourage students to expand their discussion by talking about their favorite season, what their elders do, and when they think criticism can be good.

LISTENING 2 Songkran

Before you listen

Refer students to the *Holiday activities* box. Generate a discussion about the different activities in the box. Brainstorm questions that might be asked about each, for example: *What do you usually cook for the meal? What do you wear? Where do you usually go out to eat? Do you bring gifts when you visit relatives? What kind of parade is it? Where can you watch fireworks?*

Background information

The Thai festival of Songkran happens between the 13th and 15th of April every year. Traditionally, people doused each other in water to symbolically cleanse them of any bad behavior. Splashing water was also used during Songkran to pay respect and wish people good luck. However, today it's evolved into a wild, nationwide water fight. There are lots of photos and videos of this festival on the Internet.

Global listening

Before playing the audio, ask students to try to predict the order the lecturer speaks about the topics. Then play the audio and ask students to check their answers.

AUDIO SCRIPT 2.30

Good morning, class. Today, we're going to continue our look at the cultures of South and Southeast Asia. I want to talk today about a holiday in Thailand called Songkran. Many people simply call it Thai New Year. This holiday is celebrated from April 13th to 15th. Songkran is during a very hot time of year in Southeast Asia, at the end of the dry season. People all over the country celebrate this important holiday. There are many places to experience this holiday. For example, many people visit the northern city of Chiang Mai. There, it continues for six days.

In the past, during Songkran most people visited their elders. This includes family members, friends, and neighbors. For many people, Songkran is a time to stop any bad behavior and try to do only good things. How do they do this? Well, people throw water at each other because this washes away the bad. Water symbolizes cleanliness, and many Thais clean their homes at this time. They also dress in new clothing to welcome the New Year.

Many people celebrate the holiday in a traditional way, but today it can seem the main tradition of Songkran is throwing water just for fun. People on the streets carry water and throw it onto others. They throw water on pedestrians as well as people driving by on motorbikes and in cars. It can seem like one giant water fight! Some people criticize this. They feel the origins and past traditions of the holiday are now lost. But it clearly remains a very special holiday for Thais, young and old, no matter how they celebrate it. On the last day, on April 15th, people in places like Chiang Mai walk through the crowded streets, and sing and dance. They wish Happy New Year to all they meet.

This festival is also celebrated in neighboring countries, such as Laos, Myanmar, Cambodia, and by some people in southern China and northern Vietnam. It's also celebrated in South Asia, in parts of India, Bangladesh, and Sri Lanka. In these countries, it has a different name, and people celebrate it more traditionally, and less like a fun water fight.

ANSWERS

1 when Songkran is celebrated
2 who in Thailand celebrates Songkran
3 how Songkran was celebrated in the past
4 how Songkran is celebrated today
5 why some people criticize Songkran
6 Songkran in other countries

Close listening

1 Before playing the audio, check students can remember the meaning of each symbol and abbreviation. Then play the audio and ask students to complete the notes.

AUDIO SCRIPT 2.31

Good morning, class. Today, we're going to continue our look at the cultures of South and Southeast Asia. I want to talk today about a holiday in Thailand called Songkran. Many people simply call it Thai New Year. This holiday is celebrated from April 13th to 15th. Songkran is during a very hot time of year in Southeast Asia, at the end of the dry season. People all over the country celebrate this important holiday. There are many places to experience this holiday. For example, many people visit the northern city of Chiang Mai. There, it continues for six days.

In the past, during Songkran most people visited their elders. This includes family members, friends, and neighbors. For many people, Songkran is a time to stop any bad behavior and try to do only good things. How do they do this? Well, people throw water at each other because this washes away the bad. Water symbolizes cleanliness, and many Thais clean their homes at this time. They also dress in new clothing to welcome the New Year.

ANSWERS

1 SE	4 &
2 Apr	5 b/c
3 e.g.,	6 =

2 This free note-taking practice may prove challenging to students, so you might want to play the audio twice.

AUDIO SCRIPT 2.32

Many people celebrate the holiday in a traditional way, but today it can seem the main tradition of Songkran is throwing water just for fun. People on the streets carry water and throw it onto others. They throw water on pedestrians as well as people driving by on motorbikes and in cars. It can seem like one giant water fight! Some people criticize this. They feel the origins and past traditions of the holiday are now lost. But it clearly remains a very special holiday for Thais, young and old, no matter how they celebrate it.

On the last day, on April 15th, people in places like Chiang Mai walk through the crowded streets, and sing and dance. They wish Happy New Year to all they meet.

This festival is also celebrated in neighboring countries, such as Laos, Myanmar, Cambodia, and by some people in southern China and northern Vietnam. It's also celebrated in South Asia, in parts of India, Bangladesh, and Sri Lanka. In these countries, it has a different name, and people celebrate it more traditionally, and less like a fun water fight.

3 As students complete this task, encourage them to refer to the notes in exercises 1 and 2.

ANSWER
Pictures a and c show Songkran in Thailand.

Over to you

After students have discussed the questions, invite volunteers to report their ideas back to you. Try to encourage students to give reasons each time.

Extra research task

Ask students, in groups, to find information from the Internet about a New Year celebration in another culture. This information could be used for a presentation.

Vocabulary skill

Before you ask the students to read the *Identifying word families* box, write the following words on the board:

discuss	discussion
educate	education
teach	teacher

Elicit what is common in each column. When you have elicited the concept of verbs and nouns, then write the following on the board:

_____	enjoyment
calculate	_____
_____	leader

Have students complete the blanks. Refer them to the *Identifying word families* box.

1 Ask students to work in pairs to complete the chart. Then check the answers with the class.

ANSWERS

Verb	Noun	Verb	Noun
behave	behavior	harvest	harvest
celebrate	celebration	honor	honor
clean	cleanliness	prepare	preparation
decorate	decoration	settle	settler
experience	experience	symbolize	symbol

2 After students have circled the correct words, have them choose three of the words and write sentences using a different form of the word. Invite volunteers to read out their sentences, each student using a different word.

ANSWERS
1 decorate	5 behave
2 preparation	6 cleanliness
3 symbol	7 celebration
4 settle	

3 Invite pairs to report back on their discussion to the class.

EXTENSION ACTIVITY

Write the following sentences on the board and ask students to complete the sentences:

1 How do you _____ traditional festivals in your country? (celebrate)

2 Do you _____ your house for any celebrations? (decorate)

3 What do you do before your main celebrations to _____? (prepare)

4 What _____ represent your festivals? (symbols)

After students have completed the sentences, ask them to work with a partner and discuss the questions.

SPEAKING Presenting about a special day

Grammar

Before asking students to read the *Grammar* box, write the quantifiers on the board in the wrong order and put a line from 0% to 100%. Ask the class to put the quantifiers in order.

Before asking students to complete the sentences, ask them to tell you what they can see in the picture and describe what the people are doing.

ANSWERS
1 Most	4 A lot
2 All	5 Some
3 Not many	6 None

Pronunciation skill

Write the word *of* on the board and ask students to pronounce it. Then pronounce it yourself with each of the quantifiers and ask students if they can hear a difference. Then ask students to read the *Reduction of of after quantifiers* box.

1   Play the audio twice. The first time, have the students fill in the blanks; the second time, ask the students to repeat the sentences aloud.

AUDIO SCRIPT 2.33
1 A lot of people celebrate New Year's Day.
2 Most of the students are preparing for that exam.
3 None of her classmates are absent today.
4 Not many of these photos are of this year's festival.

ANSWERS
1 A lot of	3 None of
2 Most of	4 Not many of

2   Encourage students to use a range of quantifiers to complete the sentences.

3   As students work with their partners, monitor their pronunciation and drill afterwards as necessary.

Speaking skill

Before asking students to read the *Summarizing information* box, write the four expressions from the box on the board, then elicit what all the phrases have in common.

1   Before playing the audio, ask students to read each expression from the *Summarizing information* box aloud to check their pronunciations. Then play the audio and have students complete the sentences.

AUDIO SCRIPT 2.34
1 In brief, I'll summarize the three main points.
2 To sum up, there are five dates to remember.
3 In short, we see that this holiday is fun for both adults and kids.
4 To summarize, Thanksgiving is a special holiday in the United States.

ANSWERS
1 In brief, I'll summarize the three main points.
2 To sum up, there are five dates to remember.
3 In short, we see that this holiday is fun for both adults and kids.
4 To summarize, Thanksgiving is a special holiday in the United States.

2   If students find this task difficult, choose another paragraph to practice with. For example, they could summarize a previously written essay.

ANSWERS
Main points:
On April 1st
people play tricks
France/Italy – "April fish!"
Sample summary: April 1st is April Fools' Day. On this day in France and Italy, people stick pictures of fish on people's backs.

SPEAKING TASK

After students have read the presentation and completed the exercise, ask them to work in pairs to rewrite the summary. As an extension to this task, ask students to guess what might have been said in the earlier part of the presentation.

ANSWERS
… and so there are <u>many</u> things that people can do on Earth Day. <u>Most</u> people recycle. <u>Many</u> people plants trees. <u>Some</u> people pick up garbage. <u>A lot of</u> people even use public transportation that day.
<u>Some</u> of my friends find things around the house and try to reuse them. For example, they find an old paper bag and then decorate it. They then reuse it as a gift bag! That's just one creative idea on Earth Day.

So on April 22, please remember Earth Day. In fact, as <u>many</u> people say, "Let's make every day Earth Day."
To summarize, <u>most</u> countries now celebrate Earth Day on April 22nd—about 192 in total! It's a day to increase awareness of the Earth's natural environment.

Brainstorm and plan

Before asking students to create their own mind map, draw a mind map on the board. As a class, fill in the mind map using a well-known holiday or special day. Then ask students to create their own mind maps.

Have the students plan their presentation. Explain to students that their presentations should be around one or two minutes long. Emphasize that there should be a clear beginning, middle, and end, and that they will need at least two, maybe three, main points.

Speak and share

Many students now have cameras on their phones. If it is culturally appropriate, ask students to record each other as they practice their presentations with a partner. They could then watch themselves back to see their own strengths and weaknesses.

For the *Share* task, if appropriate, students can present their ideas using supporting technology, such as through word/mind map website applications (search using *mind map app*). During this stage, monitor and take language notes. Use the photocopiable *Unit assignment checklist* on page 97 to assess the students' speaking.

STUDY SKILLS Dealing with exam stress

Background information

Many countries have acknowledged that exams can be a stressful situation for students. A variety of methods to assess students have been tried to ease the burden of stress. For example, giving more marks for coursework, or making courses modular so that the exams are smaller and regular, rather than a lot of pressure at the end of a two or three year course. You could discuss with students the system in their country, and whether they think it is positive or negative for stress and learning.

Getting started

After students have discussed the questions with a partner, come together as a class and write some of the ideas that students have for question 2 on the board. You could add any of your own tips as well.

Scenario

Give students time to read the scenario and make suggestions for Micah. Help students with any problem words. Have a whole-class discussion to share ideas.

POSSIBLE ANSWER

It isn't a good idea to cram, as it can make people feel even more stressed. It is better to have a long-term revision strategy. Micah also needs to set realistic targets. It is de-motivating to set targets that are too high. He should focus on answering the questions to the best of his ability, not on the grade. He should reward himself no matter how happy he feels. If he has worked hard, he deserves the reward. Taking regular breaks is good, and doing something he likes will help, but it is all about the balance between work and play. Rewards are a good motivator. Thinking positively helps, too.

Consider it

Ask students to read and discuss the tips in pairs. A number of answers to the questions are possible.

POSSIBLE ANSWERS

1 before
2 before
3 before/during
4 before/after
5 before/during/after
6 before
7 during
8 before/during/after
9 before/during

EXTENSION ACTIVITY

Ask students to discuss these questions related to the tips:

1 What rewards you give yourself?
2 What do you do to relax when you are stressed?
3 What do you do to distract yourself?
4 What positive thoughts do you think?
5 What other advice do you have about exam stress?

Over to you

Ask students to discuss the questions in pairs and then share with the class any other tips they have to deal with exam stress.

Extra research task

Ask students to research on the Internet other ways to deal with exam stress. In addition, if this is your last class, you could ask students to find websites that they can use to continue to practice their English.

Useful language

apps
/æps/

blogging
/ˈblɒgɪŋ/

chatting online
/tʃætɪŋ ˈɒnlaɪn/

crafts
/kræfts/

fashion
/ˈfæʃ(ə)n/

fitness
/ˈfɪtnəs/

gaming
/ˈgeɪmɪŋ/

photography
/fəˈtɑgrəfi/

social networking
/ˈsəʊʃ(ə)l ˈnetˌwɜrkɪŋ/

volunteering
/ˌvɑlənˈtɪrɪŋ/

Skillful Foundation Listening & Speaking Teacher's Book.
This page is photocopiable, but all copies must be complete pages.
Copyright © Macmillan Publishers Limited 2013.

artistic /ɑrˈtɪstɪk/	funny /ˈfʌni/
intelligent /ɪnˈtelɪdʒənt/	organized /ˈɔrgəˌnaɪzd/
sporty /ˈspɔrti/	eyes /aɪz/
hair /her/	short /ʃɔrt/
skin /skɪn/	tall /tɔl/

Skillful Foundation Listening & Speaking Teacher's Book.
This page is photocopiable, but all copies must be complete pages.
Copyright © Macmillan Publishers Limited 2013.

Unit 3 Discussion point, question 1 (p.27)

✂

city /ˈsɪti/	country /ˈkʌntri/
landmark /ˈlændˌmɑrk/	plastic /ˈplæstɪk/
ornament /ˈɔrnəmənt/	scene /sin/
snowglobe /ˈsnoʊgloʊb/	souvenir /ˌsuvəˈnɪr/
traditional clothes /trəˈdɪʃən(ə)l kloʊðz/	vacation /veɪˈkeɪʃ(ə)n/

Skillful Foundation Listening & Speaking Teacher's Book.
This page is photocopiable, but all copies must be complete pages.
Copyright © Macmillan Publishers Limited 2013.

barbecue /ˈbɑrbəˌkju/	curry /ˈkʌri/
fast food /fæst fud/	noodles /ˈnud(ə)lz/
pasta /ˈpɑstə/	pizza /ˈpitsə/
soup /sup/	steak /steɪk/
stew /stu/	sushi /ˈsuˌʃi/

Skillful Foundation Listening & Speaking Teacher's Book.
This page is photocopiable, but all copies must be complete pages.
Copyright © Macmillan Publishers Limited 2013.

Useful language

✂

assignment /əˈsaɪnmənt/	busy /ˈbɪzi/
chore /tʃɔr/	exercise /ˈeksərˌsaɪz/
grocery shopping /ˈɡroʊs(ə)ri ˈʃɑpɪŋ/	laundry /ˈlɔndri/
music lesson /ˈmjuzɪk ˈles(ə)n/	sports practice /spɔrts ˈpræktɪs/
study /ˈstʌdi/	work /wɜrk/

Skillful Foundation Listening & Speaking Teacher's Book.
This page is photocopiable, but all copies must be complete pages.
Copyright © Macmillan Publishers Limited 2013.

beach
/biːtʃ/

business district
/ˈbɪznəs ˈdɪstrɪkt/

fountain
/ˈfaʊnt(ə)n/

gallery
/ˈgæl(ə)ri/

historic site
/hɪˈstɒrɪk saɪt/

old town
/oʊld taʊn/

park
/pɑrk/

shopping mall
/ˈʃɑpɪŋ mɔl/

monument
/ˈmɑnjəmənt/

theme park
/θim pɑrk/

UNIT 8

Useful language

adults
/əˈdʌlts/

children
/ˈtʃɪldrən/

teenagers
/ˈtinˌeɪdʒərz/

old people
/oʊld ˈpip(ə)l/

young adults
/jʌŋ əˈdʌlts/

boring
/ˈbɔrɪŋ/

entertaining
/ˌentərˈteɪnɪŋ/

exciting
/ɪkˈsaɪtɪŋ/

fun
/fʌn/

mindless
/ˈmaɪn(d)ləs/

Skillful Foundation Listening & Speaking Teacher's Book.
This page is photocopiable, but all copies must be complete pages.
Copyright © Macmillan Publishers Limited 2013.

Unit 9 Discussion point, question 1 (p.87)

cook
/ˈkʊk/

exercise
/ˈeksərˌsaɪz/

homework
/ˈhoʊmˌwɜrk/

meet friends
/mit frends/

movie
/ˈmuvi/

relax
/rɪˈlæks/

shopping
/ˈʃɑpɪŋ/

sport
/spɔrt/

study
/ˈstʌdi/

work
/wɜrk/

Skillful Foundation Listening & Speaking Teacher's Book.
This page is photocopiable, but all copies must be complete pages.
Copyright © Macmillan Publishers Limited 2013.

business /ˈbɪznəs/	car /kɑr/
children /ˈtʃɪldrən/	company /ˈkʌmpəni/
education /ˌedʒəˈkeɪʃ(ə)n/	get married /get ˈmerɪd/
vacation /veɪˈkeɪʃ(ə)n/	house /haʊs/
money /ˈmʌni/	travel /ˈtræv(ə)l/

Skillful Foundation Listening & Speaking Teacher's Book.
This page is photocopiable, but all copies must be complete pages.
Copyright © Macmillan Publishers Limited 2013.

decorate /ˈdekəˌreɪt/	eat /it/
fireworks /ˈfaɪrˌwɜrks/	get together /get təˈgeðər/
parade /pəˈreɪd/	picnic /ˈpɪknɪk/
play /pleɪ/	relax /rɪˈlæks/
sleep /slip/	visit /ˈvɪzɪt/

Skillful Foundation Listening & Speaking Teacher's Book.
This page is photocopiable, but all copies must be complete pages.
Copyright © Macmillan Publishers Limited 2013.

Unit assignment checklist

Student name: _____

Date: _____

Unit assignment: Interviewing a classmate

25 points: Excellent achievement. Student successfully fulfills the expectation for this part of the assignment with little or no room for improvement.

20 points: Good achievement. Student fulfills the expectation for this part of the assignment, but may have a few errors or need some improvement.

15 points: Satisfactory achievement. Student needs some work to fulfill the expectation for this part of the assignment, but shows some effort.

5 points: Poor achievement. Student does not fulfill the expectation for this part of the assignment.

	25 points	20 points	15 points	5 points
The student uses the correct forms of *be*.				
The student forms questions correctly.				
The student pronounces plural endings correctly.				

Total: _____ /75

Comments:

Skillful Foundation Listening & Speaking Teacher's Book.
This page is photocopiable, but all copies must be complete pages.
Copyright © Macmillan Publishers Limited 2013.

UNIT 2 FAMILY

Student name: _____

Date: _____

Unit assignment: Presenting your family tree

25 points: Excellent achievement. Student successfully fulfills the expectation for this part of the assignment with little or no room for improvement.

20 points: Good achievement. Student fulfills the expectation for this part of the assignment, but may have a few errors or need some improvement.

15 points: Satisfactory achievement. Student needs some work to fulfill the expectation for this part of the assignment, but shows some effort.

5 points: Poor achievement. Student does not fulfill the expectation for this part of the assignment.

	25 points	20 points	15 points	5 points
The student uses the correct possessive adjectives.				
The student asks follow-up questions.				
The student pronounces syllables correctly.				

Total: _____ /75

Comments:

Unit assignment checklist

Student name: _____

Date: _____

Unit assignment: Talking about everyday items

25 points: Excellent achievement. Student successfully fulfills the expectation for this part of the assignment with little or no room for improvement.

20 points: Good achievement. Student fulfills the expectation for this part of the assignment, but may have a few errors or need some improvement.

15 points: Satisfactory achievement. Student needs some work to fulfill the expectation for this part of the assignment, but shows some effort.

5 points: Poor achievement. Student does not fulfill the expectation for this part of the assignment.

	25 points	20 points	15 points	5 points
The student uses possessive pronouns and adjectives appropriately.				
The student asks follow-up questions.				
The student uses correct word stress and pronunciation.				

Total: _____ /75

Comments:

Skillful Foundation Listening & Speaking Teacher's Book.
This page is photocopiable, but all copies must be complete pages.
Copyright © Macmillan Publishers Limited 2013.

UNIT 4 MONEY

Student name: _____

Date: _____

Unit assignment: Role-playing a shopping situation

25 points: Excellent achievement. Student successfully fulfills the expectation for this part of the assignment with little or no room for improvement.

20 points: Good achievement. Student fulfills the expectation for this part of the assignment, but may have a few errors or need some improvement.

15 points: Satisfactory achievement. Student needs some work to fulfill the expectation for this part of the assignment, but shows some effort.

5 points: Poor achievement. Student does not fulfill the expectation for this part of the assignment.

	25 points	20 points	15 points	5 points
The student uses appropriate demonstrative pronouns.				
The student asks about and gives the correct prices for items.				
The student uses correct intonation in questions.				

Total: _____ /75

Comments:

Unit assignment checklist

Student name: _____

Date: _____

Unit assignment: Describing a favorite meal or snack

25 points: Excellent achievement. Student successfully fulfills the expectation for this part of the assignment with little or no room for improvement.

20 points: Good achievement. Student fulfills the expectation for this part of the assignment, but may have a few errors or need some improvement.

15 points: Satisfactory achievement. Student needs some work to fulfill the expectation for this part of the assignment, but shows some effort.

5 points: Poor achievement. Student does not fulfill the expectation for this part of the assignment.

	25 points	20 points	15 points	5 points
The student uses the simple present tense accurately.				
The student asks for clarification where appropriate.				
The student uses appropriate sentence stress.				

Total: _____ /75

Comments:

Skillful Foundation Listening & Speaking Teacher's Book.
This page is photocopiable, but all copies must be complete pages.
Copyright © Macmillan Publishers Limited 2013.

UNIT 6 PLAY

Student name: _____

Date: _____

Unit assignment: Interviewing a classmate about free time

25 points: Excellent achievement. Student successfully fulfills the expectation for this part of the assignment with little or no room for improvement.

20 points: Good achievement. Student fulfills the expectation for this part of the assignment, but may have a few errors or need some improvement.

15 points: Satisfactory achievement. Student needs some work to fulfill the expectation for this part of the assignment, but shows some effort.

5 points: Poor achievement. Student does not fulfill the expectation for this part of the assignment.

	25 points	20 points	15 points	5 points
The student uses prepositions of time accurately.				
The student reacts appropriately.				
The student uses appropriate intonation patterns in their reactions.				

Total: _____ /75

Comments:

Skillful Foundation Listening & Speaking Teacher's Book.
This page is photocopiable, but all copies must be complete pages.
Copyright © Macmillan Publishers Limited 2013.

Unit assignment checklist

Student name: _____

Date: _____

Unit assignment: Describing and giving directions to a place

25 points: Excellent achievement. Student successfully fulfills the expectation for this part of the assignment with little or no room for improvement.

20 points: Good achievement. Student fulfills the expectation for this part of the assignment, but may have a few errors or need some improvement.

15 points: Satisfactory achievement. Student needs some work to fulfill the expectation for this part of the assignment, but shows some effort.

5 points: Poor achievement. Student does not fulfill the expectation for this part of the assignment.

	25 points	20 points	15 points	5 points
The student uses the modal verb *can* accurately.				
The student uses signal words accurately.				
The student links sounds effectively.				

Total: _____ /75

Comments:

Skillful Foundation Listening & Speaking Teacher's Book.
This page is photocopiable, but all copies must be complete pages.
Copyright © Macmillan Publishers Limited 2013.

UNIT 8 FUN

Student name: _____

Date: _____

Unit assignment: Discussing likes and dislikes

25 points: Excellent achievement. Student successfully fulfills the expectation for this part of the assignment with little or no room for improvement.

20 points: Good achievement. Student fulfills the expectation for this part of the assignment, but may have a few errors or need some improvement.

15 points: Satisfactory achievement. Student needs some work to fulfill the expectation for this part of the assignment, but shows some effort.

5 points: Poor achievement. Student does not fulfill the expectation for this part of the assignment.

	25 points	20 points	15 points	5 points
The student uses *so* and *neither* appropriately.				
The student correctly uses expressions for talking about likes and dislikes.				
The student uses stress in short responses.				

Total: _____ /75

Comments:

Unit assignment checklist

Student name: _____

Date: _____

Unit assignment: Inviting people to do things with you

25 points: Excellent achievement. Student successfully fulfills the expectation for this part of the assignment with little or no room for improvement.

20 points: Good achievement. Student fulfills the expectation for this part of the assignment, but may have a few errors or need some improvement.

15 points: Satisfactory achievement. Student needs some work to fulfill the expectation for this part of the assignment, but shows some effort.

5 points: Poor achievement. Student does not fulfill the expectation for this part of the assignment.

	25 points	20 points	15 points	5 points
The student uses *verb + infinitive* phrases accurately.				
The student makes, accepts, and declines invitations appropriately.				
The student correctly pronounces *have to*.				

Total: _____ /75

Comments:

Skillful Foundation Listening & Speaking Teacher's Book.
This page is photocopiable, but all copies must be complete pages.
Copyright © Macmillan Publishers Limited 2013.

UNIT 10 CELEBRATION

Student name: _____

Date: _____

Unit assignment: Presenting about a special day

25 points: Excellent achievement. Student successfully fulfills the expectation for this part of the assignment with little or no room for improvement.

20 points: Good achievement. Student fulfills the expectation for this part of the assignment, but may have a few errors or need some improvement.

15 points: Satisfactory achievement. Student needs some work to fulfill the expectation for this part of the assignment, but shows some effort.

5 points: Poor achievement. Student does not fulfill the expectation for this part of the assignment.

	25 points	20 points	15 points	5 points
The student uses appropriate quantifiers.				
The student uses appropriate expressions to begin summarizing.				
The student reduces *of* after quantifiers.				

Total: _____ /75

Comments:

Skillful Foundation Listening & Speaking Teacher's Book.
This page is photocopiable, but all copies must be complete pages.
Copyright © Macmillan Publishers Limited 2013.

UNIT 1 Self

Vocabulary preview 1

1

1 full	3 middle	5 title	7 initials
2 first	4 family	6 short for	8 nickname

LISTENING 1 Nice to meet you

Global listening

1 c	2 b	3 a	4 c

Close listening

1

1 a	3 a	5 b	7 b
2 b	4 b	6 a	8 b

2

1 student	3 call	5 from	7 full
2 interests	4 study	6 first	8 last

Vocabulary preview 2

1

1 app	3 color	5 book	7 comic book
2 TV show	4 actor	6 author	8 website

LISTENING 2 Student of the month

Global listening

1 his name	4 sports
2 his major	5 books
3 his hometown	6 movies and TV shows

Close listening

1

1 F	3 F	5 T
2 T	4 T	6 F

2

1 What's your major?
2 What is your hometown?
3 What are your other interests?
4 What kinds of books do you like?
5 Are you a fan of travel shows?

Vocabulary skill

1

1 boy	3 watch	5 baby	7 country
2 tooth	4 person	6 knife	8 woman

2

1 parents	3 dishes	5 cities	7 lives
2 potatoes	4 children	6 men	8 days

3

F	A	M	I	L	I	E	S	Y
E	N	E	S	A	Y	R	I	N
E	U	N	T	J	M	H	R	S
T	O	S	W	E	H	E	P	I
O	C	H	I	L	D	R	E	N
C	L	I	V	E	S	O	O	G
B	O	X	E	S	G	E	P	E
S	D	I	S	H	E	S	L	R
A	B	G	C	I	T	I	E	S

SPEAKING Interviewing a classmate

Pronunciation skill

1

/s/	/z/	/ɪz/
apps	bags	boxes
desks	fans	classes
parents	kinds	edges
	lives	matches
	teachers	

3

A: What are your interests, Lisa?
B: I read a lot on weekend**s** /z/. I like novel**s** /z/.
A: I have three box**es** /ɪz/ of old book**s** /s/. Do you want them?
B: Sure. Thank you!
A: I only read magazine**s** /z/.
B: What kind**s** /z/?
A: I like to read about sport**s** /s/, movie**s** /z/, and video game**s** /z/.

Grammar

1

1 Are	2 Am	3 Is	4 Is	5 Are

3

1 Where are you from?
2 What is your family name?
3 What day is today?
4 Who is your best friend?

Speaking skill

1

1 repeat that
2 your hometown again
3 please say that again
4 your middle name again

SPEAKING TASK

1 What is your full name? Amina Omara
2 Do you have a nickname? no
3 Where are you from? Tripoli, Libya
4 What is your favorite color? red
5 Do you like sports? yes
6 What are your favorite sports? basketball and tennis
7 Do you like comic books? yes
8 What is your favorite video game? Final Fantasy

STUDY SKILLS Understanding classroom language

Getting started

1 T	4 T	7 E	10 E
2 S	5 T	8 T	11 T
3 S	6 E	9 T	12 S

Scenario

Possible answer:

Francisco understands and can respond to many questions in English. He makes a note of classroom language. He also practices classroom language with a partner. However, he should try to respond in English even when his partner doesn't speak in English.

UNIT 2 Family

Vocabulary preview 1

1

1 father	4 mother	7 brother
2 son	5 sister	8 husband
3 wife	6 daughter	

LISTENING 1 Tell me about your family

Global listening

1 c	2 a	3 b

Close listening

1

1 a	2 a	3 a	4 b	5 b	6 a

2

1 b, e	2 c, f	3 a, d

Vocabulary preview 2

1

1 d	3 c	5 f	7 h
2 a	4 b	6 g	8 e

2

1 your uncle
2 your aunt
3 your niece
4 your grandmother
5 your sister/sister-in-law
6 your cousin

LISTENING 2 All in the family

Global listening

1

people in the family, where they perform, their performance schedule

2

their free-time activities, their costumes, life on the road

Close listening

1

1 T	3 T	5 T	7 F
2 F	4 F	6 F	8 T

2

The Hansen family perform for ten months a year. They perform outdoors from June to September. In October and November, they perform indoors, at places like basketball games and on boats. They also perform indoors from March to May. In December and January, they don't perform. They relax, and see their friends and family.

Vocabulary skill

1

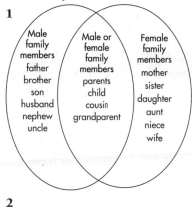

Male family members
father
brother
son
husband
nephew
uncle

Male or female family members
parents
child
cousin
grandparent

Female family members
mother
sister
daughter
aunt
niece
wife

2

grandfather — grandmother

father — mother   uncle — aunt

me   brother   sister   cousin

SPEAKING Presenting your family tree

Grammar

1

1 Her	3 My	5 Your	7 his	
2 Their	4 Our	6 Its		

2

1 Its	4 our	7 her	10 my
2 my	5 your	8 my/our	11 your
3 my	6 my/our	9 their	12 my

Pronunciation skill

1

1 2; un/cle	7 2; ques/tions
2 1; wife's	8 2; ac/tor
3 2; hus/band	9 1; blue
4 2; nie/ces	10 3; grand/pa/rent
5 3; col/le/ges	11 1; school
6 3; i/ni/tials	12 2; cou/sin

Speaking skill

1
1 What's his major?
2 Do you live with your parents?
3 What's her name?
4 What's she like?
5 What's his favorite book?
6 Where is he from?
7 How often do you see them?
8 Where does your cousin go to school?

SPEAKING TASK

1

My name is Kevin. I have a large family. I live with my parents. My father is an engineer. His name is George. My mother is a nurse. Her name is Carol. I have two sisters. One is a university student. She's 21. Her name is Dana. Her major is European history. My other sister is Jennifer. She and her husband live near us. Their son is named Peter. I like my nephew a lot. He's

---

very funny. My grandmother lives with us. She's my father's mother. She's seventy years old.

STUDY SKILLS Working with others

Scenario

Possible answer:

Amina likes to work with others and to listen to others while she is working. However, she doesn't contribute much to the discussion, and she prefers not to work with people who have very different ideas. In addition, her group doesn't collaborate with others.

UNIT 3 Stuff

Vocabulary preview 1

1

1 i	4 g	7 j	10 e
2 a	5 c	8 f	11 l
3 k	6 d	9 b	12 h

LISTENING 1 Something special

Before you listen

3
a a (baseball) cap
b a (cell/smart) phone
c a (black) (leather) wallet
d a stuffed animal/cat
e a watch

Global listening

1 e	2 d	3 b	4 a	5 c

Close listening

1 expensive; (about) 50
2 cat/animal; grandfather
3 book bag; (really) cool
4 game; sports
5 Italy; money

Vocabulary preview 2

1

1 c	3 b	5 h	7 f
2 d	4 a	6 e	8 g

2

1 organized	5 reminder
2 on time	6 messy
3 hurry	7 full
4 planner	8 folders

LISTENING 2 Get organized

Global listening

Picture a: Tip 4
Picture b: Tip 7
Picture c: Tip 2

Close listening

1

1 day	5 book bag
2 hurry	6 colored
3 planner	7 highlighters
4 reminders	

2

Sentence a: Tip 4
Sentence b: Tip 7
Sentence c: Tip 1
Sentence d: Tip 5
Sentence e: Tip 2
Sentence f: Tip 6
Sentence g: Tip 3

Vocabulary skill

1

1 organized = adj.; late = adj.; hurry = v.
2 sometimes = adv.; into = prep.; reminder = n.
3 messy = adj.; I = pron.; on = prep.
4 get = v.; full = adj.; important = adj.

2

		Part of speech	Definition
1	She's in a terrible state.	noun	a condition
2	Please state your name.	verb	to say clearly
3	Let's head to class	verb	to go
4	My head hurts.	noun	the top of the body
5	It's past your bedtime.	adverb	after
6	Forget the past.	noun	the time before now

SPEAKING Talking about everyday items

Grammar

1

1 yours	3 his	5 theirs	7 ours
2 mine	4 mine	6 yours	

Pronunciation skill

1 feature	4 supplies	7 organized
2 review	5 reminder	8 stapler
3 engineer	6 highlight	9 expensive

Speaking skill

1
1 What's it called?
2 How do you say that in English?
3 What's the word for it in English?

2
1 an opal (necklace)
2 a (stuffed) hedgehog
3 a beret

SPEAKING TASK

I have a special item. It's a statue of a cat. It's from Japan. It's from my parents' trip there. It's called *maneki neko* in Japanese. You see them in front of restaurants, banks, and offices. I believe they welcome people. I think they are good for business. My sister has one, too. I keep mine in my bedroom, and she keeps hers in her office at work. I think it's really cute!

STUDY SKILLS Creating a vocabulary notebook

Scenario

Possible answer:

Adding and removing pages can be good as you can get rid of pages with words you now know. However, it is unlikely that a student will know all words on one page at the same time, so cards with individual words on might be better. Topics are a good way to organize words. Collocations usually help students improve their vocabulary more rapidly. Translations are less likely to help Ana learn words than writing definitions, as it requires less mental effort. The lack of example sentences means Ana could struggle to move from a passive understanding to an active use.

UNIT 4 Money

Vocabulary preview 1

1

1 b	3 c	5 b	7 b
2 c	4 a	6 c	8 a

LISTENING 1 Can I help you?

Before you listen

S Can I help you?
S What size?
E Thank you.
C How much is it?
E Here you are.
S It looks nice on you.
S Cash or charge?
C Do you have it in black?
C Where is the fitting room?

Global listening

	Section	What they are shopping for
1	fashion accessories	perfume
2	sporting goods	basketball, tennis racket
3	jewelry	necklace/jewelry
4	women's clothing	black blouse / gift for wife (and electronics)

Close listening

1 first	3 15	5 six	7 ten
2 third	4 34	6 18	8 second

Vocabulary preview 2

1

1 on sale	5 purchase
2 bargain	6 exchange
3 tag	7 receipt
4 discount	8 refund

LISTENING 2 Weekend sales

Global listening

1 jewelry and fashion accessories
2 electronics
3 sports equipment and clothing
4 furniture

Close listening

1 a	3 b	5 a	7 a
2 a	4 b	6 b	8 a

Vocabulary skill

1

1 difficult	3 large	5 similar
2 happy	4 near	6 fast

2

1 kids	5 carpet	9 speak
2 shop	6 couch	10 begin
3 present	7 get	11 choose
4 cab	8 end	12 purchase

SPEAKING Role-playing a shopping situation

Grammar

1 What's that? It's a necktie.
2 What are these? They're earrings.
3 What are those? They're sneakers.
4 What's this? It's a tennis racket.

2

1 ✓
2 **These** shoes hurt my feet. I need to sit down.
3 Listen to **this** podcast. Do you like it?
4 ✓
5 **Those** children in the other apartment are noisy!
6 Please put the books here. **This** is my desk.

Pronunciation skill

1

Speaking skill

1

1 $69.50
2 $112
3 $97.25
4 $1.50
5 $89.99

SPEAKING TASK

Conversation 1

Salesclerk: Can I help you?
Customer: Yes. How much is this shirt?
Salesclerk: It's twenty dollars.
Customer: What size is it?
Salesclerk: It's a medium.
Customer: Oh.
Salesclerk: Do you want to try it on?
Customer: No, that's OK. Where is the sporting goods section?
Salesclerk: It's on the fourth floor.

Conversation 2

Salesclerk: Can I help you?
Customer: Yes. How much are these sunglasses?
Salesclerk: They're $12.
Customer: Do you have them in blue?
Salesclerk: No, I'm sorry. But those sunglasses over there come in blue.
Customer: Oh, those are nice. How much are they?
Salesclerk: They're $169.
Customer: Um, I'll keep looking.

UNIT 5 Taste

Vocabulary preview 1

1

1 e	4 f	7 k	10 b
2 h	5 l	8 i	11 d
3 j	6 a	9 g	12 c

LISTENING 1 Mealtime habits

Global listening

	Breakfast	Lunch	Dinner
Spain		✓	
Japan			✓
Russia		✓	
Oman		✓	

Close listening

1 People drink ~~tea~~ **coffee** with milk for breakfast.
2 *La merienda* is eaten before ~~lunch~~ **dinner**. / *La merienda* is eaten ~~before~~ **after** lunch
3 Breakfast is rice, fish, soup, and ~~black~~ **green** tea.
4 For lunch, ~~beans~~ **noodles** and rice dishes are popular.
5 Breakfast is small and ~~slow~~ **fast**.
6 Fish ~~heads~~ **eggs** are popular.
7 People have ~~yogurt~~ **bread** with tea or coffee for breakfast.
8 ~~Milk~~ **Fruit** is popular at night.

2

1 between 9:00 and midnight/12 a.m.
2 between noon/12 p.m. and 1:00
3 between 7:00 and 8:30
4 between noon/12 p.m. and 3:00

Vocabulary preview 2

1

1 sour	6 juicy
2 salty	7 creamy
3 spicy	8 chewy
4 bland	9 crispy
5 sweet	10 oily

LISTENING 2 Street food

Global listening

1 d	3 c	5 f
2 e	4 a	6 b

Close listening

1

1 Brazil	4 Jamaica
2 the Philippines	5 Canada
3 Germany	6 South Africa

2

1 soft, chewy, sour
2 sweet, creamy
3 chewy, salty
4 spicy, juicy
5 crispy, oily, salty
6 crispy, spicy

Vocabulary skill

1

1 sugary	4 bony
2 cheesy	5 crusty
3 buttery	6 fatty

2

1 oil	4 juice
2 taste	5 spice
3 cream	6 salt

3

1 bony	4 fatty
2 crusty	5 cheesy
3 sugary	6 buttery

SPEAKING Describing a favorite meal or snack

Grammar

1

1 Where do you eat in your home?
2 Do people in your country eat a big lunch?
3 Why do people like to eat street food?
4 What time does dinner start?
5 Does fruit have a lot of sugar?
6 Does your teacher allow snacks in class?

2

Possible answers:

1 Where do you eat lunch?
2 What time do you have lunch?
3 Why does he like nuts?
4 Where does Pam have lunch (every day)?
5 How often do they eat oatmeal for breakfast?
6 What does Ben never drink at night?

Speaking skill

1

1 What does "couch potato" mean?
2 What exactly do you mean?
3 I don't follow.
4 Can you explain that?

Pronunciation skill

1 and 2

1 A: He is a <u>bad egg</u>.
  B: I <u>don't</u> <u>follow</u>.
  A: He is a <u>bad person</u>.
2 A: An <u>apple</u> a <u>day</u> <u>keeps</u> the <u>doctor</u> <u>away</u>.
  B: <u>What</u> do you <u>mean</u>?
  A: <u>Fruit</u> is <u>good</u> for you. It <u>keeps</u> you <u>healthy</u>.

SPEAKING TASK

Lara: My favorite snack is nachos. Nachos are crunchy tortilla chips, cheese, beans, meat, and salsa.
Rani: Salsa? Can you explain that?
Lara: Salsa is a spicy mix of tomatoes, onions, and chilies.
Rani: That sounds good.
Lara: I don't order nachos in restaurants. I like to make my own at home. I make them when we watch movies with friends. We usually drink soda with them. I like nachos because they are cheesy and delicious, and they're easy to share with friends.
Rani: Are they healthy?
Lara: Um, I don't think so.

STUDY SKILLS Using a learner's dictionary

Scenario

Possible answer:

Some people argue that bilingual dictionaries are not ideal learning tools for learners, as it doesn't take much effort to understand something that is simply translated. Arguably, though, at a low level they can be helpful. George uses the bilingual dictionary to support him rather than as his main dictionary, which is advisable. However, he should also use a learner's dictionary at home.

UNIT 6 Play

Vocabulary preview 1

1 play sport	5 read
2 run	6 walk
3 cook	7 chat online
4 watch TV	8 play video games

LISTENING 1 A typical day

Before you listen

Belgium has the most free time.

Global listening

1 c	2 b	3 c	4 b

Close listening

1

1 b	3 b	5 b	7 a
2 b	4 a	6 b	8 a

2

1 Sophie has classes in the afternoon.
2 Colin prefers team sports.
3 Kumiko is a sociable person.
4 Eduardo is single.

Vocabulary preview 2

1

1 c	4 f	7 h
2 a	5 e	8 i
3 b	6 d	9 g

LISTENING 2 What a hobby!

Global listening

1

1 c	2 d	3 a	4 b

Close listening

1 bilingual	3 gifts	5 brother	7 GPS
2 58	4 mother	6 parts	8 sign

Vocabulary skill

1

go: bowling, jogging, skating, swimming
play: badminton, the guitar, tennis
do: aerobics, taekwondo, yoga

SPEAKING Interviewing a classmate about free time

Grammar

1

in: 1999, the afternoon, September, the spring
at: 10:15, night, noon
on: 06/24/2013, December 12th, Friday, the morning of May 1st, New Year's Day

Speaking skill

1

1 a	2 b	3 a	4 a	5 a

Pronunciation skill

1

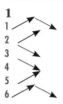

SPEAKING TASK

Interviewer: Do you have a lot of free time?
Keltoum: No, not really. I only have about three free hours a day.
Interviewer: That's too bad. On a typical day, what do you do in your free time?
Keltoum: Well, I like to play computer games. I play with my friends.
Interviewer: Oh yeah? When do you play? Do you play in the afternoon?
Keltoum: No, we play at night. We play on weekdays.
Interviewer: That's interesting. Where do you play?
Keltoum: I usually play in my bedroom.
Interviewer: So what else do you do in your free time?
Keltoum: I collect seashells. I have about 500 of them.
Interviewer: Wow! That's amazing! Why do you collect seashells?
Keltoum: I don't know. They're just beautiful, I guess.

STUDY SKILLS Doing a web search

Scenario

Possible answer:

Tanya only needs to type "English learner dictionary" (and inside quotation marks) in her first web search. The fewer the words used, the more accurate the search. In her second web search, she is right to put the book title in quotation marks, but she should also include the year of publication for a more precise search. In her third web search, it is good that she uses the minus sign to exclude what she does not want to search. However, it is not good practice to use the first information she finds on the web. She should ask herself questions such as *Who wrote this? Are they an expert? When was this written? Is it academic?* She should then double-check the information on at least one more website.

UNIT 7 Places

Vocabulary preview 1

1

1 b	4 a	7 a
2 a	5 b	8 b
3 b	6 a	9 a

LISTENING 1 Is it far?

Global listening

1

1 c	2 a	3 e	4 d	5 b

2

1 near	2 near	3 far	4 near	5 far

Close listening

1 bus stop (on Fourth Avenue, next to school)
2 bookstore (on corner of First Avenue and Maple Street, next to stationery store)
3 train station (on corner of Elm Street and Fourth Avenue, next to tech store)
4 ATM (on Second Avenue, next to drugstore)
5 post office (on corner of Elm Street and Third Avenue, next to supermarket)

Vocabulary preview 2

1

1 market		5 aquarium
2 theater		6 tower
3 zoo		7 amusement park
4 botanical garden		8 stadium

LISTENING 2 New to Australia

Global listening

1 Opera House
2 Harbor Bridge
3 Royal Botanical Gardens
4 Taronga Zoo
5 Sydney Tower
6 State Theater

2

7 Queen Victoria Building
8 Sydney Aquarium
9 Fish Market
10 Olympic Stadium
11 Luna Park
12 Bondi Beach

Close listening

1 a	3 b	5 b	7 b
2 a	4 b	6 a	8 b

Vocabulary skill

1

1 adj.; e		4 n.; a
2 v.; f		5 v.; d
3 n.; b		6 adj.; c

2

1 buy paper		5 watch sports
2 get money		6 see fish
3 borrow books		7 see a play
4 buy groceries		8 see animals

SPEAKING Describing and giving directions to a place

Grammar

1

1 can	3 can't	5 Can	7 can't
2 Can	4 can't	6 can't	8 can't

Speaking skill

1 first	3 X	5 after that
2 then	4 next	6 X

3

1 We're at the corner of Oak Street and Second Avenue.
2 Walk up Second Avenue.
3 Go straight until you get to Elm Street.
4 Take a right at Elm Street.
5 Walk down Elm until you see a tech store and a hair salon.
6 Walk a little more.
7 The train station will be on your right.

Pronunciation skill

1

1 It's on your right.
2 Walk about ten minutes.
3 You can't miss it.
4 Can I help you?
5 Go to Second Avenue.
6 Can you give me some information?

SPEAKING TASK

A: Do you ever go to the video arcade in this neighborhood?
B: No.
A: It's a cool place. You can play some really fun games there. You can also get food and drink there if you want.
B: Really? Where is it exactly? Can you give me directions?
A: Sure. First, walk down the small street by our school. Follow it for about ten minutes. Then turn right at the big tech store. Do you know the one?
B: Yeah.
A: After that, walk about two more minutes. You will see a small street on the left. Go down that street until you see the arcade. It's on the first floor. You can't miss it.
B: Great! I can't wait to go.

UNIT 8 Fun

Vocabulary preview 1

1

1 c	4 f	7 h
2 b	5 d	8 i
3 a	6 e	9 g

LISTENING 1 I miss that show!

Global listening

1

1 b	2 d	3 a	4 c

Close listening

1

1 F	3 F	5 F
2 T	4 T	6 T

2

1 –	3 –	5
2	4	6 –

Vocabulary preview 2

1

1 c	3 a	5 e	7 f
2 d	4 b	6 h	8 g

2

1 garbage		5 escalator
2 arcade		6 deep
3 bin		7 fall
4 experiment		8 theory

LISTENING 2 The fun theory

Global listening

1

You can change people's behavior by making things more fun.

2

1 b	2 c	3 a

Close listening

1

1 Swedish		4 points
2 Not many		5 20
3 glass		6 in a park

3

1 c	2 b	3 b

Vocabulary skill

1

1 A polar ~~bare~~ bear spends some of its life on the ice.
2 Walk ~~threw~~ through the park, and then take a right.
3 You can ~~by~~ buy four tickets for a dollar at the video arcade.
4 Let's ~~meat~~ meet by the escalator inside the main doors of the mall.
5 Hurry to the department store because everything is on ~~sail~~ sale.
6 The new ~~rode~~ road to my high school is blocked by snow today.

2

1 hi; high		5 eight; ate
2 guest; guessed		6 here; hear
3 add; ad		7 wait; weight
4 there; their		8 right; write

SPEAKING Discussing likes and dislikes

Grammar

1

1 so is Susan
2 so do I
3 so does my husband
4 neither are my friends
5 neither do her sisters
6 neither does my best friend

2

1 does	**3** am	**5** are
2 do	**4** is	**6** do

Speaking skill

1

1 Luke likes reality shows a lot.
2 I don't like sitcoms at all.
3 I hate watching game shows.
4 Rex doesn't like watching TV very much.
5 Shannon loves to download TV shows.
6 I like reading novels very much.

Pronunciation skill

1

1 Really? <u>I</u> do.
2 So do <u>I</u>.
3 <u>Neither</u> do <u>I</u>.
4 Oh? <u>I</u> don't.

SPEAKING TASK

A: Let's watch TV. Sound good?
B: Sure. What do you want to watch?
A: How about Sunday Nights Sports? I love that show.
B: Really? I don't. I find it boring. But I love to watch soccer.
A: So do I. But there's no soccer on—just baseball.
C: Life with Mickey is on. I like that show.
A: Oh? I don't. I don't find it funny at all. But I like that reality show Super Student.
C: So do I.
B: Can we watch a documentary? I see that Extreme Journeys is on. I love that show.
C: I don't like it at all. Sorry.
A: Neither do I.
B: It's not easy to agree on anything.
C: Why don't we go outside and do something? We can go to the park.

STUDY SKILLS Prioritizing tasks

Scenario

Possible answer:

Ling is doing a number of things correctly. Firstly, she is making a list of things to do. She is also prioritizing her tasks and thinking about deadlines. Unfortunately, she does not think carefully about how long each task will take and so does not have enough time. Additionally, it is a mistake to do the easy things first. She should make the important things a priority.

UNIT 9 Plans

Vocabulary preview 1

1

1 b	**3** a	**5** c	**7** c
2 c	**4** d	**6** d	**8** b

LISTENING 1 My plans

Before you listen

1 tonight
2 tomorrow morning
3 tomorrow afternoon
4 tomorrow night
5 the day after tomorrow
6 this weekend
7 next weekend
8 next month

Global listening

Michelle ✗

Jasper ✓

Ashley ✓

Saito ✗

Close listening

1

Michelle: **1** bowling **2** parents **3** tennis **4** movie

Jasper: **1** dinner **2** baseball **3** mall **4** skiing

Ashley: **1** museum **2** drive **3** barbecue **4** hiking

Saito: **1** shopping **2** house **3** Spanish **4** dinner

2

1 tonight
2 tonight at seven
3 tomorrow night
4 at 2:45

Vocabulary preview 2

1

1 wash the dishes
2 do the laundry
3 buy groceries
4 take out the garbage
5 water the plants
6 clean the house
7 pay the bills
8 put away the groceries

LISTENING 2 Are you free?

Global listening

1 join a study group
2 go bowling
3 attend a talk
4 plan a project
5 visit a museum

Close listening

1

1 decline
2 accept
3 decline
4 accept
5 decline

2

1 I need to do the laundry tonight.
2 I have to clean the house.
3 I have to study for a test.

Vocabulary skill

1

1 movie theater
2 hair salon

3 stationery store
4 graduation dinner
5 tennis player
6 video arcade
7 bus station
8 amusement park

2

SPEAKING Inviting people to do things with you

Grammar

1

1 to wash	**5** to have
2 to see	**6** to buy
3 to do	**7** to study
4 to go	**8** to book

2

1 What do you plan to do this weekend?
2 What grade do you hope to get in this class?
3 Do you need to do any chores today?
4 Do you have to study this evening?
5 Where would you like to travel someday?

Speaking skill

1

Conversation 1

1 A: Are you free tonight?
2 B: Yeah. I think so.
3 A: Do you want to go see Super Drive 3 at the Green Theater?
4 B: Thanks. I'd love to.
5 A: Great. Is the 7:00 show OK?
6 B: Sure. Let's meet at the theater.

Conversation 2

1 A: Would you like to go to a baseball game tonight?
2 B: What time is the game?
3 A: At 7:00 this evening.
4 B: Sorry, I can't. I have to meet my study group.
5 A: That's too bad.
6 B: Maybe some other time.

SPEAKING TASK

A: Are you free on Tuesday afternoon?
B: Yes, I am.
A: Do you want to work on our class project?
B: Sure. I'd love to. What time?
A: How about at 3:00?
B: That sounds good.
C: Are you busy on Saturday?

D: A little. Why?
C: Would you like to go to the museum?
D: What time?
C: At 1:30.
D: I'm sorry, but I can't. I have to study at the library then.
C: That's OK.

UNIT 10 Celebration

Vocabulary preview 1

1

1 c	3 e	5 a	7 j	9 i
2 d	4 b	6 h	8 g	10 f

LISTENING 1 Thanksgiving

Global listening

1 f 2 d 3 c 4 e 5 a 6 b

Close listening

1

1 &	3 w/	5 e.g.,	7 4th
2 =	4 b/c	6 1st	8 etc.

2

1 &	3 b/c	5 =	7 w/
2 4th	4 1st	6 etc.	8 e.g.,

3

Possible answers:

1 It's in fall because that's when the harvest is celebrated.
2 They knew how to farm, hunt, and fish well.
3 Their meal was meat, corn, and different types of shellfish.
4 They decorate their homes and have a large meal with their family. Sometimes they watch football games on TV.

Vocabulary preview 2

1

1 b	3 a	5 a	7 a
2 a	4 b	6 b	8 a

LISTENING 2 Songkran

Global listening

1 when Songkran is celebrated
2 who in Thailand celebrates Songkran
3 how Songkran was celebrated in the past
4 how Songkran is celebrated today
5 why some people criticize Songkran
6 Songkran in other countries

Close listening

1

1 SE	3 e.g.,	5 b/c
2 Apr	4 &	6 =

3

Pictures a and c show Songkran in Thailand.

Vocabulary skill

1

Verb	Noun	Verb	Noun
behave	behavior	harvest	harvest
celebrate	celebration	honor	honor
clean	cleanliness	prepare	preparation
decorate	decoration	settle	settler
experience	experience	symbolize	symbol

2

1 decorate	5 behave
2 preparation	6 cleanliness
3 symbol	7 celebration
4 settle	

SPEAKING Presenting about a special day

Grammar

1 Most	3 Not many	5 Some
2 All	4 A lot	6 None

Pronunciation skill

1

1 A lot of	3 None of
2 Most of	4 Not many of

SPEAKING SKILL

1

1 In brief, I'll summarize the three main points.
2 To sum up, there are five dates to remember.
3 In short, we see that this holiday is fun for both adults and kids.
4 To summarize, Thanksgiving is a special holiday in the United States.

2

Main points:
On April 1st
people play tricks
France/Italy – "April fish!"
(Students' own summary)

SPEAKING TASK

… and so there are many things that people can do on Earth Day. Most people recycle. Many people plant trees. Some people pick up garbage. A lot of people even use public transportation that day.

Some of my friends find things around the house and try to reuse them. For example, they find an old paper bag and then decorate it. They then reuse it as a gift bag! That's just one creative idea on Earth Day. So on April 22, please remember Earth Day. In fact, as many people say, "Let's make every day Earth Day." To summarize, most countries now celebrate Earth Day on April 22nd--about 192 in total! It's a day to increase awareness of the Earth's natural environment.

STUDY SKILLS Dealing with exam stress

Scenario

Possible answer:

It isn't a good idea to cram, as it can make people feel even more stressed. It is better to have a long-term revision strategy. Micah also needs to set realistic targets. It is de-motivating to set targets that are too high. He should focus on answering the questions to the best of his ability, not on the grade. He should reward himself no matter how happy he feels. If he has worked hard, he deserves the reward. Taking regular breaks is good, and doing something he likes will help, but it is all about the balance between work and play. Rewards are a good motivator. Thinking positively helps, too.